Praise for *The American Dream Is a Mindset*

"Bill Lombardo has written a book sales people will find invaluable, full of firsthand stories of sales success and handy tips for forging your own path in the industry."
—Daniel H. Pink, *New York Times* best-selling author of *To Sell is Human, Drive,* and *Whole New Brain*

"Bill Lombardo has taken what we have learned about hundreds of millions of years of human brain evolution and applies it to a winning strategy for sales. Digging deeply into the human psyche, he has come up with a fresh and revolutionary look at success in the sales industry."
—Dr. Rudolph E. Tanzi, Joseph P. and Rose F. Kennedy Professor of Neurology, Harvard Medical School; Vice Chair of Neurology and Director of the Genetics and Aging Research Unit at Massachusetts General Hospital/HMS; coauthor with Deepak Chopra of *Super Brain* and *Super Gene*; TIME Magazine 100 Most Influential People in the World

"I have known Bill Lombardo as a sales coach, author, and corporate training leader on the highest level. Bill has cracked the code on how any salesperson can reach peak performance by optimizing mindset. This is a must-have blueprint to meaningful success in sales and sales leadership."
—Jon Tota, Cofounder and President of Edulence

"To live the American Dream, as Bill Lombardo says, requires skills and mindset. The more important of these is mindset and this can be learned. This book will help you not only to succeed but also to

become a successful person so that everything you do is continually done better. Read this book to make your entire life better. I admire Bill and you will too."
—Jim Cathcart, CSO, CPAE; international speaker; author of *Relationship Selling, The Eight Competencies of Relationship Selling: How to Reach the Top 1%,* and the newly released *The Self Motivation Handbook*

"Bill Lombardo clearly identifies fearless qualities and models that can truly have an impact on all leaders and their teams. With his thirty years of experience across industries, the application of these strategies can only enhance 'fearless leaders across the insurance/sales pipeline.'"
—Dr. Cathy Greenberg, *New York Times* best-selling author; coauthor of *Fearless Leaders: Sharpen Your Focus*

"This book is a must read for anyone who wants to be successful in sales or wishes to create a work environment where salespersons excel, find meaning in their work, and outperform their wildest dreams. This inspiring book uses practical applications, examples, and stories to develop self-leadership, sales approaches, and techniques. It truly does show the sales rep how to build a 'Mindset for Success,' become a more effective sales leader, and engage with secrets to higher sales performance."
—Dr. Glenn Boseman, CLU, CLF, RICP; Bingay Professor of Leadership and Dean, Irwin Graduate School, The American College of Financial Services

"There are two attributes that successful sales professionals possess: passion and a rock-solid belief about why they are in this career. Bill addresses the importance of both—passion and why—in a manner that only a person truly engaged in the success of others can communicate."
—Frank Sarr, President of Training Implementation Services, Inc.

THE AMERICAN DREAM IS A MINDSET

*Proven Strategies to Hardwire Your Brain
for Great Sales and Leadership Success!*

BILL LOMBARDO

Contents

To Mrs. Mary Lou Manning, the teacher all students need and wish for, and Danielle Coucke Lombardo, my special life partner whose support and inner strengths make this book possible.

MY STORY

Ihave been a student of selling and leadership for more than thirty years. This book is my legacy and a tribute to all who sell and who develop leaders for a living.

I have worked for established corporations such as Ford Motor Co., Owens-Illinois, Inc., and Bankers Life as well as groundbreaking startups such as Princeton Learning and eMind. Through it all, I have learned a lot about selling and leading, and earned valuable experience in some unexpected ways.

My career started simply as a marketing representative with a packaging company. Or you could say I was a salesperson selling boxes. Nothing in my MBA program prepared me for this role other than the knowledge that through hard work I could achieve most goals.

I was fortunate. I had a great sales manager who became my mentor and role model. He shared with me his basic behavioral sales techniques such as smiling more, accepting a coffee when offered, and acting as though I was visiting a friend when on a sales call. It went without saying that when you took a purchasing agent to lunch you needed to handle at least two drinks—and it was usually Scotch back then!

My sales manager modeled good business ethics and took me to the plant that produced the boxes I was hired to sell. He pointed out that without my selling, the plant employees would be jobless and might not be able to provide for their families. He was trying to help me understand that there was real meaning and purpose in my work.

But there was no sales training program per say. No sales development, let alone sales strategies. It was the Marines storming the beach approach back then—get tough, work your way through all obstacles, and win the business!

Leadership was for the most part all about the charismatic boss giving directives—one person giving the organization all they needed to know. Thankfully, Peter Drucker, "father of modern-day management" was on the scene and provided us with insights into management and leadership that were otherwise sorely missing.

Sales work is not easy and definitely not for everyone. Over the years, the field has improved significantly with companies now offering more structured training programs. It turns out that knowledge is the differential. Knowledge of better sales skills and of the products or services offered.

Before, the salesperson had knowledge that the consumer didn't. Training was based on this concept: leveraging the salesperson's obvious advantage over prospective customers. But not so today. With a more level playing field now, the salesperson is no longer the gatekeeper of information. And a sales call or meeting is no longer a scripted event. So much of the interaction now needs to be extemporaneous and reliant on improvisation, depending greatly on how one reads and then connects with the other person.

I have watched many good sales candidates who possessed all of the "old school" required skill sets—a warm personality, a good communication style, a strong work ethic—fail. Their training was seemingly adequate but in truth it did not embrace what early on was on the fringes and even now is largely embraced only by early adopters. That is their training didn't provide enough tools for developing a critical "Mindset for Success" and truly connecting with others.

Dramatic changes are now taking place and that is why I felt compelled to write this book. We are beyond just the early adoption stage but not yet mainstream. Meaning, this place in between what was before high risk to what is now a steady movement toward low risk offers you great opportunity to jump ahead of the pack today. And I'm not just talking to real estate agents, insurance brokers, product reps, and others generally thought of as being in professional sales.

Daniel Pink, in *To Sell Is Human*, says it so well: *"10% of the population is directly involved with sales and the other 90% are and don't know it."*

Lawyers sell to clients, doctors sell to patients, teachers sell to students, managers sell to their teams and employees and bosses, parents sell to their children—all trying to reach agreement, to persuade and influence others to change their minds and take certain actions.

We are all selling and leading in some form in our different roles. Selling and leading are a necessity today for reaching success in any role or profession. As a result, strong sales abilities are gaining in stature and demand as we look to the future. This need for selling skills in all professions is highlighted by the increase in undergraduate and graduate programs with sales courses.

The internet is a major driver in this movement. Today, knowledge is available to the buyer as easily as it is to the seller. Whether it's about comparing prices and features, or confirming availability and delivery times, the seller-buyer relationship has been forced to change. Now, selling is about building relationships, meeting needs, and delivering high quality.

Mindset Is the Key

Neurologists are now able to observe, using fMRI technology, what parts of the brain we must operate in to achieve peak performance. This is exciting news with more to come from further research. From here we can learn to better guide our thoughts, emotions, and actions and thus raise our level of performance and sense of fulfillment in our careers and personal lives.

My fifteen years of work in leading, establishing, and building learning networks for two major financial services corporations taught me something very important: there is a significant crossover in skill sets for those who sell and those who lead. In fact, as you read this book, I will freely interchange between discussing selling and leading. Just as I have smoothly interchanged between training and developing thousands of sales agents and doing the same with thousands of managers.

Currently, as an Executive Leader Coach, I apply insights I learned from a multiyear study I conducted. I profiled, interviewed, and applied the "360 Assessment" tool with the very best sales professionals and leaders. This provided me with an understanding of what they are made of and what makes them stand out from the rest. Findings from my study have also been validated by the emerging advances in neuroscience and have resulted in me developing proven models and techniques that can be used to manage a "mindset for success," as well as to build healthy relationships with prospective and existing clients and colleagues.

Yes, the study reveals that the very same set of interpersonal skills that orient toward better self-understanding, which in turn helps one influence others to change their thinking or to take action, can be applied to those in sales and those in leadership positions.

With this book, I want to share with you the **<u>Sauce</u>** that positions these people—they are ordinary people like you and me—to achieve extraordinary performances and results. One ingredient is they know their WHYs that fuel their inner beliefs—like hard work, GRIT, self-determination, and strong personal values. This sauce can give you a *system of proven* Models and Techniques to take your game to the next level and achieve greater sales and leadership success—and yes, even greater personal fulfillment.

The American Dream Is a Mindset offers you three fundamental pillars:

I. **Greater Self-Awareness**
II. **Mindset Model and Techniques for achieving more success and fulfillment**
III. **CASA Model and Techniques for improved relationship-building and coaching skills**

People from a wide range of backgrounds, from those who hit the streets just out of high school to master's degree graduates, from those who struggled to those who were privileged, became very successful and enjoyed great fulfillment in their work and personal life as a result of the approach you will read about in the upcoming pages. And a number of their personal stories are included as well. Ones that I believe will resonate with you.

There are many questions nowadays about the American Dream and whether or not it still exists. Well, what I know as fact, and what this book substantiates, is that indeed the American Dream is alive, well, and thriving. I know this because the American Dream is a mindset. It always has been and always will be. It's a belief that the human potential is limitless. That when we're truly helping others we are in that mindset. That this generosity of spirit also results in greater personal achievement and fulfillment.

But please don't mistake this to be one of those books promising **A New You** to solve your problems. What I promise you, though, is an **opportunity** to be inspired and guided by proven strategies that can help shift your mindset toward greater success.

Bill Lombardo
August 1, 2018

Chapter 1
A Story of Transformation

The commute from Plymouth to Boston wasn't too bad, at least not at first. The scenery was pretty, especially during the fall when the change of seasons in New England was so inspiring. As the landscape changed, so did people's spirits in anticipation of new beginnings. The high-end health club where Lori Moncada was general manager was state of the art with all of the equipment and services you might expect from a popular spot with the locals. There were men and women of all ages climbing the hill to get toned while others were already winning at being in shape. It made Lori feel good that she was doing something that had meaning behind it. And it was fun. At least for a while until she began to feel stuck. A while. Yes. And not just for what she could call only a transition because that stuck feeling went on for years.

"Lori, doing alright?" coworkers started asking.

"Yeah, sorry I was just thinking about something. I'm okay. What's up?" She knew how others could put up good fronts—probably like a lot of the fancy clientele she served at the health club did—and now she found herself perfecting the art of illusion too. Behind her bright smile and trim waistline, a battle inside was unfolding. Her negative self-talk was starting to escalate, which only added to her already pressure-filled life. Thoughts about not being good enough, smart enough, pretty enough, or anything else enough kept running through her mind.

She was constantly beating herself up too for not being home with her family, for missing moments with her young children, and worrying how she was going to keep a balance between their needs and the demands of her job and financial responsibilities.

But she held on, until she couldn't. She felt her grip slipping away in dealing with the often persnickety clientele who bordered on being over-the-top at times. Then there was pressure from the home office. The execs were positioning the clubs for sale and their focus was solely on the bottom line. Keeping up member satisfaction along with employee satisfaction, then squeezing out every drop to show stronger earnings became an almost impossible task.

Problems mounted and she started feeling like she didn't have time to breathe. The hollow pit in her stomach lasted from morning to night. And then even through the night, tossing and turning, moving from the bed, to the guest bedroom, to the couch in search of a place to lay her head and fall asleep. "I felt like a failure," she says in describing that period. In most cases her persistence served her well, but at some point her tenaciousness began working against her. Her focus narrowed into tunnel vision. And from those cramped quarters, answers seemed to narrow down too. "I didn't think making a change was an option. I didn't think I had the ability to do better anywhere else." She would say to her spouse, "We've got the bills. And how are we going to save for the kids to go to college?"

With three adopted children to raise, feed, and love, her job had forced her out of the life she had known and she needed it back. Her three little ones made her sense of purpose more clear. So if not for herself, then for her children, she had to make a change.

But still more time passed with Lori stuck. The drive to Boston, once a kind of sanctuary for her inner thoughts to rise, had become more of a hell. The loneliness of the road. The loneliness of the twenty-four-hours a day, seven days a week constancy of her job. The loneliness of getting home too exhausted to play with the kids. Until finally, after ten years of doing this, it all became too much.

Lori went back to her roots of personal training and found her way into management consulting. The hours were better, the pay so-so, but it was invigorating and intellectually challenging in ways that made her feel better about herself. She could be home with the family. They could have dinner together. Have some laughs. Watch some TV. Be normal like other families. Lori didn't know it then, and only years later was she able to look back and realize that this was the turning point when the clouds began to lift and her confidence began to grow more.

And then one afternoon at work she got a phone call. She didn't know the woman on the other end of the line. She said she saw Lori's resume posted on Monster.com and that's how she got her number. "Anyway Ms. Moncada, I'm in the insurance business," she started. And from there she invited her to a career briefing. Had she called years earlier, it wouldn't have been the right fit. But now, it might be. It occurred to Lori that had she not allowed herself to leave the familiar and place herself in a position for more growth, she could have missed this opportunity. Lori wondered about what else she may have missed out on by not being more open. She wondered if other people were like her in struggling to break free, struggling against the currents, until finally feeling like they could reach the shore. Actually, she was very hesitant to attend the insurance "thing." Mostly because of the stigma associated with being an insurance agent. It was a roadblock for her and honestly, she toyed with skipping out on this meeting. But something inside told her to go, that there was something there for her. She thought that her instincts about this were strong, so it was better to follow them than wonder "what if?"

This decision turned out to be a game changer! Lori became one of the most successful agents in the company's history. She was the number one agent for three years in a row and among the top three agents over the last seven years.

You may be asking how Lori went from being stuck, to being in transition, to becoming so successful? It wasn't, as you might imagine, when "one door closes and another opens." It was more like one door was pried open enough to at first see some light come through, then pried farther to get a hand through, and then a leg through, until finally she pushed it open enough to get out.

Her start in insurance sales was filled with setbacks and disappointments. She had constant fears. That she wouldn't hit her numbers. That people would judge her as being less than because she had to pull a rabbit out of a hat each month to make ends meet. That some of the clients she was trying to sell to, with their nice homes, their brimming 401Ks, their BMWs, their kids with trust funds would see right through her. "What do I amount to?" she'd ask herself.

It turns out she had what money alone can't buy: "grit"—a level of self-determination that left her knowing that whatever the challenges were, she would learn from them and grow. And that success would come with time and experience, regardless of her modest station in life.

Graduating with a master's degree in exercise physiology from San Diego State University, life had led her across the country to the east coast. Always searching for what felt right, lost perhaps in her direction, but nevertheless determined to find her true north, she persevered and put her energies into not only being successful at sales but also into understanding the why and the how of it all. For Lori it came down to the basics—arrived at by peeling back the layers to reveal her genuineness.

"I don't really know that I do anything or behave any differently than anybody else or have any attributes that nobody else has," she said. "I approach the whole business from my heart and I do have the ability to build relationships with clients. I think that's where my success stems from. But I also think and feel that anyone who is willing to work hard, become a student of this business, and truly believe they are helping their clients will be successful."

The relationship building—yes, of course, she already knew that from early on. From work at the health club too. It was instinctive. Even back in college, she knew that allowing for vulnerability to be present and being accepting of others without judgment might be called "people skills" in the business world, but for her it was just living her life as she knew how to. Not being one to conform so easily, her path to individual identity gave her the chops to stand up for what she believed in, while at the same time gave her the understanding that good people can have disagreements. People who love each other can argue. People who dislike each other can find common ground. These were life lessons she picked up as she went along.

Taking it all into account, the way of her heart is the way of her career. Integrity, determination, and resilience—they are values she lives up to, no matter who she is sitting across from. In reality then, Lori's life integrates closely into her work and her work integrates closely into her life. It's not a job. It's a love. Sometimes she thinks it's corny, but she says it anyway, "It's a calling." Helping other people is what she's about. It's what ties everything together. Facing her fears every day, staying disciplined every day, and staying committed every day really comes down to also fulfilling her own need to help others. Because Lori has already seen what it means to work for a paycheck, she now is able to work for having a greater vision about life, service, meaning, and purpose, in addition to providing security for her family.

She sits quietly in her kitchen, looking out the window into the backyard. The trees are beautiful. The shrubs need trimming and weeds need to be pulled. But still, it's home—a refuge from the demands of success. "How can I improve?" she asks herself as steam floats up from her cup of hot coffee. The peanut-buttered toast takes her attention for a moment and then back into quiet reflection she goes. It's just her nature.

Living with a higher sense of self-awareness is her path. The same discipline and commitment she shows to her work, she also shows to her personal enrichment. Meditation and affirmations are fundamental to both.

Lori has come to live an outward life that is consistent with her inward life. The result is her self-respect translates into showing respect for others. The compassion she shows herself is conveyed equally through compassion for others. The nurturance and soothing comfort she gives herself to keep her stress manageable, she passes forward to others to help them ease their jitters. The calmness she has in setting intentions to achieve her goals, she spreads to helping others reach theirs.

Another sip of coffee as her thoughts focus on having a clear mind. She places a premium on this clarity. It helps her communicate with people effectively. It helps her be present in the moment. It helps her set boundaries with those she may have difficulties with. And it helps her have fun.

After all, sales work is not meant to be tedious. The joy in helping people and the joy in connecting with others moves her forward. Rather than being the always-serious overachiever, Lori balances the positives with the hardships. Through her naturally optimistic view, she sees opportunity where challenges arise. In fact, those challenges are fertile ground in which she envisions growth possible. If something is bothering her, she confronts it, believing that it is bothersome for a reason and she wants to understand that reason because she's not content to push it aside, any more than she would push aside a friend needing to talk.

This drive toward self-improvement and helping others is a guiding principle. She says she thinks of it as "an expression of my integrity. Anyway, how else could I live my life?" It's what she knows. It's who she is. With this self-knowledge comes a feeling of freedom from the weight of constant changes, the constant pull on her time and having to prioritize only to later have to reprioritize.

She gets up from the kitchen table and rinses her coffee cup and breakfast plate. Then places them in the dishwasher. The one certainty she can count on is a sense of being centered with herself. The kids are still asleep. The house is quiet. It's both special and ordinary at the same time....

Lesson Learned

Lori Moncada is one of the most successful insurance agents in the nation. This story shows how you, or anyone else, can apply the basic principles of increasing self-awareness, building strong relationships, overcoming setbacks and fears, and maintaining discipline as a formula to reach your own goals. Success can be defined in many ways, but certainly consistently demonstrating these traits can bring you a rewarding life, however you choose to measure rewards.

A lot has changed since Lori started as a sales professional. Yet, she remains one of her company's top agents partly because she is flexible enough to adapt to change. Now, more than a decade after she joined the business in 2005, the overall sales workforce has become filled with increasingly more highly skilled, smart, caring, sensitive, ambitious people. Ones who value listening and ones who know the value of building relationships. Ones who know that forcing a sale will likely come back to haunt them and that beating the pavement day after day is no match for building up a loyal following that trusts you and relies on you for your service. And most important, that change is a constant.

So why am I pointing out what you could probably learn yourself on the streets? One of the reasons is to help put you on the fast track to adapting to changing environments. Another is to help you succeed more on your terms, rather than moving with the way the wind blows. And a third reason is to help you better help others—those older and younger and those you see as your peers—in a time calling for innovative ways to move forward with cooperation and synergy.

Chapter 2
See and Believe

Whether you were born on first base or third base, are high-school educated or hold an advanced degree, a stutterer or an eloquent speaker, woman or man, gay or straight, single, divorced, or married, white, black, or yellow, immigrant or native, the question for all is how can you live up to your fullest potential? Granted, some have an easier time than others. But what I do know too is that finding opportunity and seizing it is also a major factor in the equation. It's not just genetic predisposition and it's not just hard work or good luck. You also have to be able to read the landscape.

This book is designed to help you see opportunities more clearly. And first among those opportunities is an understanding that leadership starts with each of you. Don't wait for a change or a lucky break to take charge of your direction. You already have the authority to do this. Just find the opportunities that can serve as vessels to carry you forward.

This book is also designed to give you a system with the latest thinking, models, and techniques to achieve greater sales and leadership success. For example, the following are three proven keys I'll be discussing and emphasizing throughout this book:

1. The critical importance of developing greater **self-awareness and the ability to direct your thoughts and "rewire" your brain.**

2. The critical importance of developing **significant relationship-building skills.**
3. The critical importance of understanding that you have the ability to effectively **manage and work through setbacks, anxieties, and fears.**

At the center of our present-day economic and technological revolution, with power shifting between consumers and providers, are sales—who gets them, who doesn't. Who's good, who's lucky. Who shares, who monopolizes. The revolution underway is not going to be reversed either, so I would advise you to not sit this out because selling is the lifeblood of the economy. Without it, there are no businesses. There aren't even nonprofits. Now is a time when you can become a part of this massive social movement through your own salesmanship and leadership. But first, here's a primer on what's behind this shift and then a look at where we are headed.

For starters, consumers can now counter spins by conglomerates or one-person businesses with a tweet, a YouTube video, a social media post, or a comment on any of the thousands of watchdog websites. From airlines to auto mechanics, if you interact with the public, there's likely a trail of consumer reactions about you on the internet. The posts don't even have to be deliberately aggressive. A two star out of five rating on Amazon can spell disaster for a product. What used to be reserved for the insiders, like the esteemed Michelin Guides rating restaurants and Moody's rating investment grade bonds, has now been leveled to include anybody with an opinion, whether it's an informed one or not.

I'll tell you a personal story about how this shift recently affected me. My wife, Danielle, and I were looking for a new house a few years back. I was excited for the move but dreading the process. Besides, I didn't have time to be dragged around by a realtor who I suspected would be more interested in their 2 percent commission than in my family's happiness. After all, I'm a sales guy. I know how they think.

Danielle surprised me. She went online and searched for homes in the area where we wanted to live. She took virtual tours and zoomed in on still photographs to get a closer look at details. She went on Google Maps and looked at the next-door neighbor's house and up and down the block. Then she researched online comparable sales for nearby houses—all of this before ever even contacting an agent. And when she was ready to do that, she googled some real estate agencies and looked at their websites. She checked out their customer comments posted on Yelp and other forums to see whether or not the agency was good to work with.

Danielle even googled real estate agents to see how others felt about their service and to learn more about them; she even googled about their personal lives from their Facebook pages, without ever leaving the house. Armed with all of this information, she found us a home. The agent we ultimately worked with, in truth, only facilitated the lead role my wife had already established. That agent didn't sell us a house. We bought one.

As a result of the new online advantage for the buyer, sales professionals are losing their dominance as gatekeepers of information. Their new place in the relationship with consumers is increasingly becoming one based on more equal footing. The consumer now has the power of information but still often relies on a partner—someone like you—to help guide them to the right decision and solution.

Another factor to look at in understanding how we got here is the recent Great Recession, which rained down the worst economic conditions since the Great Depression. Millions lost their jobs, their homes, and their sense of identity and had to reinvent themselves. Working in sales became an outlet for many of these displaced but motivated, professional, and dedicated individuals needing to transition into new careers. Sales offered them the opportunity for commissions and bonuses that rewarded performance. This was opposed to the guaranteed salary-based positions so many had grown comfortable with, only to have that business model collapse as companies downsized or went under.

Retail sales in particular has seen an increase in the number of mature, more experienced workers. What used to be seen as summer employment or even part-time supplementary work has now been filled with seasoned professionals. Walk into a department store and see how the face of retail has changed to reflect this step up in who works these positions. And this shift is having a significant impact on the overall economy. In fact, the retail industry is the largest employer in our nation's economy, accounting for 10 percent of the total employment. The National Retail Federation estimates their industry sustains directly or indirectly more than 15 million jobs. With these increasing numbers comes more pressure for better wages. What's significant about retail sales is that these settings are where the average American most often experiences interactions with a salesperson. These frontline workers, including those with e-tailers, are thus ambassadors for others in sales professions.

At the forefront of this new frontier is an understanding of how self-awareness influences sales professionals, and actually everybody, much more than had previously been thought. We only need to look to ancient times, for example, Socrates, who said, "An unexamined life is not worth living." Modern-day thinkers such as Daniel Goleman, a psychologist who helped popularize the discussion about "emotional intelligence," were talking decades ago about how increasing self-awareness could help people change. Today, emotional intelligence is a widely accepted term in business, along with ROI, market share, and liquidity. And it is finding even greater applications as more people embrace the concept of mindfulness to yield new choices for fulfillment and success. What was once "out there" is now mainstream.

For example, Dr. Rudolph Tanzi is a Harvard-based neuroscientist whose work on understanding the brain has earned him high praise worldwide. Specifically, he is a leader in research on neurological functioning and currently spearheads the Alzheimer's Genome Project. He is also listed by Thomson Reuters as one of the top 1 percent of researchers in the field of neuroscience. In 2015, he was included among TIME magazine's 100 Most Influential People in the World.

In his book, *Super Brain,* Dr. Tanzi brings to light how simply observing your thoughts and feelings is the essential first step to improving the quality of your life. He goes on to talk about how the evolution of the brain to move beyond just survival, beyond the two poles of pain and pleasure, is emerging to place self-awareness ahead of selfishness.

In Dr. Tanzi's words, "If you think about selfishness, that the original brain stem was fight or flight, find food and find a mate, and it was all about self, self, self, survival. It was every person for themselves. Don't worry about the community yet. Don't worry about the social interactions yet. Just survive. Find enough food, then find somebody to reproduce with and keep the species going." But now, through millions of years of evolution, "Your brain is allowing you to know you have a brain. That's what self-awareness is."

Here's the takeaway for any salesperson or leader from Dr. Tanzi's words—through self-awareness we can rewire the brain and override our genetic makeup. Tactically, we can reprogram the brain through repetitive affirmations, visualizations, and positive emotions to overcome negative thoughts and behaviors and change them to positive ones. The result can have an impact on our success.

In addition, as our senses develop so do the ways in which we have self-awareness. In fact, it is forward thinking, it is a display of leadership, to be in touch with our feelings. Having self-awareness is its own credential, in a sense like an MBA or other graduate school degree, for advancing a career. With this new knowledge, we can better adjust to working on a team, as well as improve our own individual performance.

But self-awareness is not just another commodity to buy, even though many may promise that they have the next sure thing to happiness and fulfillment. It's actually more of an education to develop a disciplined mind, courage, persistence, and a willingness to be vulnerable, among other traits. This gateway to epiphanies doesn't come easily for most people. However, there are some exercises and models described later in this book that can help. Among them are Dr. Tanzi's views on the value of repetition of positive affirmations, a good disposition, and a good outlook.

There's a story I like to tell that shows how this way of thinking can be applied to the real world. No doubt there are always skeptics who have heard all of this "attitude adjustment" stuff before. Evan Ha, a successful sales agent from Toms River, New Jersey, is a go-getter. He's disciplined, efficient, goal-oriented, and driven to succeed. He's hardly the type to get caught up in any hype, so for Evan, all of this talk about self-awareness has to measure up to the very high standards he sets for himself. And it does.

Evan has applied his gains in self-awareness to the art of listening. When he's with a client or a prospect, he tries to structure the conversation in an 80/20 ratio—that is, he listens 80 percent of the time and talks 20. His 20 percent, though, usually consists of open-ended questions that allow the other person to express more. He also applies his self-awareness to helping him get through a tough day or tough week. By knowing himself and what he responds well to, he is effective at getting his mind off setbacks and back to finishing strong. For instance, he's responsive to self-talk that touches at the core of his personality—that which reminds him of the bigger picture. In his own words, "I am doing noble work for my clients. I am helping to change their lives for the better."

This is what clicks for Evan. Someone else might be responsive to repeating specific affirmations or prayers. Another to listening to music. While another to reading. There are lots of ways to increase your self-awareness. Just find what works for you.

One of the most notable benefits you will find with increased self-awareness is a greater ability to read your relationships in business and at home. In short, **by understanding yourself more, you can understand others more and achieve greater success.**

Throughout my many years in training, development, and coaching thousands of colleagues, one of the common threads I have found among those who are most successful in sales and leadership is an emphasis on building quality relationships. In part, this is because the products or services they offer are often comparable to others. But what is not so easy to match up head to head is the quality of relationships they build with their clients and teams. For instance, if prices are the same in comparison to others, then it is the personality—the essence of the salesperson—that can determine whether a client chooses to work with that salesperson or with someone else. And if price is higher, the salesperson's essence—sense of humor, practicality, sincerity, humbleness, responsiveness, empathy—in the client's mind, can be well worth the extra cost.

In fact, a salesperson or leader is regarded as wise when he or she places the greatest emphasis on being of service to, and meeting the needs of, their client: keeping in mind the saying **"Do unto others as you would have them do unto you."** Develop a sense of gaining more business by doing right by the customer.

In *To Sell Is Human* by Daniel H. Pink, the author sets forth that the core of selling is really about being of service. He models his thinking after the concept of "servant leadership" developed by Robert Greenleaf in the 1970s. According to Mr. Greenleaf, leaders were most effective when humble rather than domineering, and when they were there to serve. Essentially, heeding a call to be of service was an indicator of a true leader.

Mr. Pink adds, "The time is ripe for the sales version of Greenleaf's philosophy. Call it "servant selling." It begins with the idea that those who move others aren't manipulators, but servants. They serve first and sell later. Pink's qualifier, similar to that for Greenleaf's, is: If the person you're selling to agrees to buy, will his or her life improve? When your transaction is over, will the world be a better place than before you began?"

Ryan Veariel, a sales agent in Houston takes this understanding to heart by making sure he puts clients' interests first. He says, "I treat each person like they are an extension of my family." This way he knows he'll be providing the best service he's capable of. When he goes into an appointment, he doesn't think about pressure to get the sale "so I can pay my bills." Instead he says, "I need to do what's right for my client. If you spend your entire time trying to make money, thinking 'I'm going to go out and write five contracts today,' you're going to end up failing because you're trying to push a product on someone they may not need."

He adds, "If you're always focused on meeting the needs of your clients and not pushing products on them, then you're going to be successful just by the nature of the business." By focusing on the number of people he can help rather than on the number of sales he needs, he's proven in his own words, "doing what's right for my client, not what's right for my wallet," what keeps him a sales leader.

This approach is also distinguished from those who, in an effort to cut costs and maximize profits, push self-service, which often puts distance between the provider and the customer. In contrast, this more sweeping approach that emphasizes customer service breeds a deeper connection. And it broadens the meaning for what is being sold. For example, it's not just a product or a service, it's also comfort or hope. This whole concept of selling has evolved to a much more sophisticated level. And though those who are aware of it may not truly be visionaries, they are at least astute at seeing opportunities where others blinded by self-absorption cannot.

This mindset is similar to one discussed in the best-selling book *Blue Ocean Strategy: How to Create Uncontested Market Space and Make Competition Irrelevant* by W. Chan Kim and Renee Mauborgne. The crux of the book is to go where others are not and stake out a niche. As it relates to sales, there's blue ocean with a customer base that is more informed than ever before, with more choices than ever before, and with more power for recourse if they are dissatisfied than ever before.

To service this base requires, among many things, a high level of ethics. Old rules such as overcoming objections are still important in successful selling, but this blue ocean calls for temperance with a healthy respect and understanding, for example, that at some point no means no. This evolution "86es" a hard-sell approach and fear tactics and instead gives way to **a culture of genuineness**. To a benevolence that together, the sales professional and client can reach a mutually beneficial understanding. One where the sales professional's power and control are swapped for being of service and for being a resource to meet the customer's needs.

You're right if you are thinking that getting ahead of this wave requires a lot of initiative. Some call it being a self-leader.

If you have the grit in you to embrace your individuality, your passion, and your talents, then you already have the capacity to see yourself as a leader with beliefs that fuel the support you need, as well as the autonomy you need, to be your best.

There's an old saying that goes "success has many fathers, but failure is an orphan." It is easy to lead when things are going well, and I'm including self-leadership here too. In fact, good fortune could come from favorable circumstances that have little or nothing to do with the leader. For instance, Mexican food found a solid base of diners beginning in about the 1950s but was mostly confined to the southwest. Decades later, now in 2018, it is a nationwide bonanza. You think pizza is popular? Guess what? Mexican restaurants just surpassed the number of pizzerias in the United States. So avocado farmers who provide for all of that guacamole aren't necessarily leadership geniuses. The market moved in their favor through no doing of their own. They're holding on to the tail of a tiger as south of the border flavors keep gaining in popularity coupled with an increasing demand for health foods.

Setbacks, though, leave little room for a leader to shrink. In this sense, with everybody being a leader and inevitably everybody experiencing setbacks, it's vital right from the start to see yourself as capable of enduring hardship and rising above it.

Each person has their own way of dealing with adversity. Notice I use the word adversity and not failure. To me, failure happens when you don't learn anything from misfortune. If you learn, and if you set your mind to growing from a hardship, then it is not a failure. It is a learning experience. Some of the greatest lessons about life are gained through facing adversity. So be bold. Fearing failure is common, but don't let that fear immobilize you.

There isn't a person on the planet who doesn't have to deal with setbacks. The difference, though, is how each of us responds to them. Assessing the situation beforehand, including weighing the risks and rewards, can help prepare you for setbacks if and when they do come. Building a support system to help you through rough times is also helpful. Being kind to yourself and understanding that you are only human, and that some adversities are out of your control and a part of life, are also good to keep in mind. And for those setbacks that you do have to own, going easier on yourself is a good step to making peace within. By recognizing your own humanness and still having the courage to continue to take calculated risks, you can help comfort yourself during difficult times, and look to the future with lessons learned to do better next time.

The same is true for fears. Everyone has fears. Every one, despite their public persona. Rather than shaming yourself for being afraid, embrace your fear. Live with it. Confront it. Come to understand its roots and, through that self-discovery, you can free yourself from the shackles of unreasonable reluctance. It is quite common to think that being afraid is a weakness, but really the opposite is closer to the truth. Your fears represent your personal experiences and perceptions. They are there to protect you from harm. Perhaps they have been in place too long. For instance, you may have been taught early on to keep quiet while the grown-ups talked. If that belief is still active in your subconscious as an adult and it holds you back from expressing yourself, then it has outlived its purpose. But that doesn't make you weak—it makes you ripe for growth.

Many people talk to family and friends about overcoming their fears. Others read books, write in journals, and recite affirmations. Some contemplate in private using a form of meditation, and increasingly more are using some form of mindfulness. Whatever method works for you, pursue your freedom vigorously because, as a sales professional or leader, you are always in some stage of dealing with the fear of rejection. To shut down or deny or put it out of your mind only gives your fears more roots. Instead, seek out ways to convert fear into self-knowledge. From there you can open yourself to more opportunity, and likely transcend even more of your fears. It is truly a measure of character to confront your fears. And from there you can better help others confront their own.

Transcending fear is also a hallmark of a successful person. Later in this book, we'll talk with sales professionals and leaders about their views on success. You'll find it's much more than money. It is a culture centered on being of service to others. The result is greater self-fulfillment that then can lead to greater financial rewards.

Included in this discussion about success are tools and exercises to help you attain your goals. For example, I'll introduce you to the Mindset for Success Model. This model shows how to help you better understand your beliefs, emotions, and actions. It works. It's based on the leadership development success I have had with hundreds of sales professionals and leaders all across this nation. By refining your thinking, you clear the path for greater rewards. It's not mystical. It's practical.

The same is true for another model named CASA, which stands for **C**onnect, **A**greement, **S**kill, and **A**ccountability. Through this model, you will learn how to connect more effectively with others, have more successful sales calls, and develop more leadership skills with an emphasis on listening and empathizing.

If you apply even a fraction of the understandings and step-by-step techniques in this book, I believe you will immediately increase your sales and improve your leadership abilities.

Chapter 3
The Power of Self-Awareness

Go in to any bookstore, turn on the television, surf the internet—everywhere you turn, you'll find people talking about "being a better you." And it's not just for the unlucky or confused, it's also now tailored as self-enrichment for the happy and accomplished who are seeking even further development. Over the last several decades, self-awareness has transformed from being a warm and fuzzy interest to having a high correlation with increased success and happiness.

In fact, many executive training courses for Fortune 500 companies as well as small businesses use building blocks from the field of developmental psychology to bolster their ranks, inspire innovation, and improve the bottom line. Actually, some of the same approaches that have been used in individual counseling by psychologists have become widely commercialized. For instance, you no longer need to go to a "shrink" to find out what motivates you. Just pick up *The Wall Street Journal,* or *Forbes* or *The Economist* and you'll find plenty of examples of leaders who publicly reveal parts of their inner psyches even though not so long ago this was considered to be best kept private. They delve into and reveal their thoughts. Not just any thoughts, but ones about what will make them a better person, a better listener, a better leader, a better spouse, or a better parent.

Dr. Glenn Boseman, Bingay Leadership Professor at the American College of Financial Services, embraces this new direction, as do many other leading-edge scholars and icons in management studies, such as John Maxwell. We say leading edge, but in truth this approach has been around for decades.

Classics like Dale Carnegie's *How to Win Friends and Influence People* published in 1936 or Nathaniel Hill's *Think and Grow Rich* published in 1937 telegraphed this transition to the business world. Now, much of the social awkwardness around you and others wanting to be more self-aware has lifted. For example, international mega-selling business books such as *Who Moved My Cheese* by Spencer Johnson, *The Tipping Point* by Malcolm Gladwell, *7 Habits of Highly*

Effective People by Stephen Covey, *Start with Why* by Simon Sinek, and many others are in essence self-help books that have crossed over to the business category. If you haven't read these or other writings like them or engaged in your own introspection, then you are not only missing out on improving your performance but you are also likely falling behind your peers—that's how widespread the science and art of self-awareness has become in commerce.

In the acclaimed book *Talent Is Overrated* by Geoff Colvin, the author describes the transition from old school business models that emphasized amassing financial capital to today's environment where human capital is equally emphasized. He explains that Microsoft and Google know quite well the value of their hires as he writes, "Bill Gates has said that if you took the twenty smartest people out of Microsoft, it would be an insignificant company, and if you ask around the company what its core competency is, they don't say anything about software. They say it's hiring. They know what the scarce resource is."

Colvin goes on to say, "For virtually every company, the scarcest resource today is human ability. That's why companies are under unprecedented pressure to make sure that every employee is as highly developed as possible."

Which leads to the new buzzword in the field of self-improvement: mindfulness. It essentially refers to being in the present moment, fully attentive to the person you are talking with or the activity you are engaged in. Along with supporting research, it has thrown cold water on the earlier notion that multitasking is the most desirable way to achieve more and be more efficient and effective. Actually, multitasking has been shown to inhibit productivity whereas mindfulness is proving to be the key to greater productivity.

So how do you become more mindful? Through self-awareness.

That means understanding how to calm your mind, live in the present moment, and focus. This can be achieved in a number of ways. One is through meditation—I know you might think this is for monks secluded in the Himalayas, but it's far from that. Meditation, contemplation, introspection, or collecting your thoughts—whatever you want to call it—is not only occurring while in caves in the Arunachala Mountain in Tamil Nadu but also while playing eighteen holes at Kayak Point in the Seattle metropolitan area, relaxing in the spa at Canyon Ranch in Tucson, or hiking through Treman Gorge to the 115-foot Lucifer Falls near Ithaca, New York. The fact is you don't need to go anywhere. Just putter around in your garden, play with your kids or grandkids, walk the dog. Even NBA legendary coach Phil Jackson and his former players Michael Jordan, Kobe Bryant, and Shaq O'Neal credit George Munford, a mindfulness teacher, with elevating their games to a higher level. Clearing your head and increasing your mindfulness can occur in many ways. Start by accepting that practicing mindfulness, in whatever way that suits you, is a worthwhile step toward greater success and fulfillment.

In addition, admitting your desire, even need, for better self-understanding is taking initiative to make yourself more effective and prepared for greater responsibility. For instance, if you are in leadership, you have to be able to inspire your colleagues to strive for excellence. To do this you must understand them; by the very nature of human behavior this means you have to understand yourself. What makes you tick? What are your vulnerabilities? What triggers set you off? What plays to your strengths?

The same is true if you are a sales professional meeting face-to-face with a client. For example, Hilda Akhamzadeh, a sales executive in Los Angeles knows that understanding her client gives her a leg up on a competitor, particularly one who may just want to get in to make the sale and get out. She says, "Building relationships is essential to my success. And in order to build, I have to understand people and understand myself." In that sense, gaining self-awareness is like other education. The more you know, the better equipped you are to take care of your responsibilities and reach your goals. Unlike at school, though, which is sometimes a place where you fill your mind with information that may or may not have relevance to your life, self-awareness education is directly applicable to your life.

In fact, every moment you invest in better knowing yourself can translate into results to improve your well-being, and, by extension, the people and principles you are devoted to.

For instance, in applying this better understanding of yourself to your career, you can better manage your stress; better respond to crises and curveballs that might otherwise throw you into a tailspin; better analyze a situation to find more creative solutions than the ones simply put in front of you; and better forecast how your clients might respond to changes in services, products, prices, or competitors. In short, self-awareness is an essential tool for success in today's climate. If you have any doubts about this, look at those who continually outperform others. Even though these successful people may not call it self-awareness that is what they engage in. For example, the expressions "he doesn't force things, but goes with the flow" or "she is good at reading people" are just other ways of saying these individuals are attuned to themselves and to others.

Along the road to gaining more self-awareness, you will undoubtedly resist uncovering your inner workings. After all, delving into the unknown can shake up your beliefs about things that you have banked on as being true, and even about what has fundamentally made you into the person you are today. Learning to deal with this resistance and finding ways to reduce it are all a part of the self-awareness process, as described later in this book. You can't simply learn to know yourself better like you might cram for an exam. Instead, it is more of a building experience, where enough self-knowledge can allow you to deconstruct old ineffective habits and reconstruct new effective ones. This takes time. But with steadiness and tenacity, you can build a solid foundation on which further grow becomes progressively easier.

One indication that this foundation is in place is a willingness to accept that changes and disappointments are a routine part of growth. You can be a catalyst for change and embrace progress or you can hold on tight to what is outdated but comfortable because of its familiarity. By recognizing how you respond to change, and by finding comfort in knowing that change is challenging for just about everyone, you can become more adaptable. That means adjusting to evolving market conditions and absorbing company strategies that flex with available financial resources, technology, talent pool, and more.

Dr. Rudolph Tanzi, who I spoke of earlier as a pioneer in brain research, and who coauthored with Deepak Chopra, MD, *Super Genes* and *Super Brain,* has an interesting take on adapting to these challenges. He says, "You are not your brain. The last four million years of evolution provides you with self-awareness. Through self-awareness you can observe and change your thoughts to rewire and reprogram your brain. Social interaction is still driven by fear and desire. So, through this greater self-awareness you can reprogram your brain to overcome setbacks, challenges, and fears."

He goes on to say, "Maturity comes with dealing with your emotions in your limbic system. But if you're hiding in your intellect all day, and then when you're not there you just jump back to your frontal cortex, and it becomes fight or flight, find food, and mate, then you are juvenile."

Perhaps there was a time when you could hide as Dr. Tanzi says, and get by with the tools and resources handed to you. But not today. Not in the fast-paced, consumer-driven, consumer-empowered economy we live in. It is not so much a choice about whether it would be wise to invest in understanding yourself better, but a choice about whether you want to be relevant. By skipping over the call for self-awareness, by not heeding the ancient wisdom of Socrates to "know thyself," you place yourself at a great disadvantage in the marketplace.

I want to be clear, though, that self-awareness is a personal, often private journey. By opening yourself up to introspection, you are not necessarily opening yourself up for public examination. This is important to keep in mind because you deserve your privacy. What you discover about yourself is for you to use as you are comfortable—it's okay either way; choose to tell others or not. The changes that come about through increasing self-awareness are oftentimes subtle, building one insight upon another, which means you can typically anticipate evolving gradually, rather than experiencing sudden dramatic change, so you're not "outed."

At sales branches throughout the nation, managers, sales teams, and administrators are embracing this new dynamic that self-awareness brings to relationships with each other and with their clients. They recognize it as a pivotal factor in professional success and personal fulfillment. For example, branch managers talk about the value of having mentors or coaches—people you can confide in and gain some valuable feedback from. People who will take time out of their own busy schedules to lend a helping hand. For these mentors, there is a sense of giving back. After all, someone helped them get to where they are so serving as a mentor is a way of passing their wisdom forward.

Through this understanding, whether as a leader or as a sales professional, you can come to know how important it is to inspire people. In fact, you might not be able to motivate others, but I strongly believe you can inspire them. Inspiring people is our job each and every day. I believe we are here to help others be the best they can be.

As a leader, sales professional, mentor, or team support member, you can foster an environment where colleagues feel safe to come forward. For example, they may express either directly or imply, "Hey I'm really scared. This challenge is really big." In a healthy environment the two of you can communicate genuinely and come up with solutions together. To paraphrase the visionary leadership expert John Maxwell, "If everything's going smoothly in your life, you're going down the hill." Simply put, if there are no challenges, you're not growing.

To grow, you're going to face difficulties that will necessitate channeling your energy into constructive solutions. The success of this process is a reflection of your level of self-awareness. So if you are going to have a "meltdown" in the face of pressure, you won't get too far. But if you can calm yourself, evaluate your options, and take appropriate action, you can push through.

Here's a story I like to tell about Farshad Asl, a sales manager in Los Angeles, and one of his young, fresh recruits who was just getting started with their company. After Farshad asked what his biggest challenge was, the young man replied, "I'm married. I have kids . . . and . . .

Farshad asked, "And?"

"I live with my parents."

Farshad didn't hesitate. "Okay. I think we can work together."

The young man became a successful new agent in the first three months that Farshad coached him. One day he came in and said, "I moved out of my parents' house."

"That's outstanding!" Farshad congratulated him.

Now he'd been married for five years, stuck in that house, and after only five months in his new job he was able to move out. In part this had to do with the coaching process deadline. Farshad encouraged him, "Give yourself a deadline. Let's come up with a goal for when you move out."

Farshad reflected back on that day: "It's just the best feeling when people come to you and say, 'You know what, thank you. I became a successful new agent. I moved out of my parents' house.' And amazingly, four months after that, this new guy came into my office.

"'Guess what?'

"I don't know. What?

"'For my wife's birthday I bought her a car.' "

Afterward Farshad said, "You know, it almost brought tears to my eyes."

So you need a dream. You need drive. And you need discipline. These all come from within. Others can help guide you and inspire you, but taking the needed action is internal. Ultimately, when you take full responsibility for the process to understand who you really are, then you can begin to experience an accelerated growth toward your fullest potential. With this greater sense of who you are, it is easier to do the right thing, largely because you have a clearer moral compass to fall back on and because you have a clearer picture of what making up excuses is all about. You still have explanations and hold others accountable, but without the excuses and blaming.

Another sales professional, Joe Veilleux from Concord, New Hampshire, has come to understand what motivates him to take action—keeping an enjoyable and balanced life. That realization resulted from an awareness about his priorities and about his limitations. Early on in life, he had wanted to be a doctor, but it turned out that he didn't have a knack for understanding biology. Instead of being shelved by this broken dream, though, he admits it was pretty shattering, he picked himself up and reinvented himself. "I figured I wanted to make a lot of money to be able to provide for my family because I knew I wanted to coach and do outside activities. Sales gave me the opportunity to do that. I've got a wife and three kids—now a son who's nineteen, a daughter who's seventeen, and a daughter who's twelve. They are my why. That's why I work hard—to provide them with the things they want."

Coaching, enjoying other activities, having time for his family, and doing meaningful work all added up for Joe based on his understanding of his priorities. Defining success for yourself means taking stock of how you want to spend your time. It is up to you to identify your course and then stay true to it. This can be especially difficult when you take a hit, or many hits.

But in Joe's view, you have to expect to take hits all through life, and life hits hard. You've got to get back up and keep going. You've got to figure out what to do next like Joe did. Being a doctor wasn't in the cards for him so he applied his self-awareness to help him persevere—to dig deep and find the grit to push through setbacks. Now he's in a leadership role and, when it comes to helping his team deal with hits, he advises they follow his example. To have this kind of candor depends on his understanding of them—in his words, "to know what makes people tick."

He also talks about the value that self-awareness adds to his leadership style. For instance, Joe has an ability to set aside one issue because another has taken priority and to stay focused even with demands coming at him left and right. And in addition to that, of course, there is life outside work to deal with. "You need to be able to compartmentalize things, deal with what you have to deal with, pick them off as you go throughout your day to accomplish something. Because otherwise it's very easy to just get weighed down."

Joe's also learned to ask for help when he needs it. By understanding sometimes he doesn't have the answers, and to not be too proud to ask for a hand, he believes he lifts himself up as a more prudent, realistic leader—one who is aware he still has room to grow as a person.

This opens the door to something a lot of people have a hard time facing. You have to be willing to learn. You have to be receptive to new ideas. You have to be tolerant of valid perspectives that are different from your own. And you have to remain dedicated to the long-range view about developing yourself. I'm sure you don't need me to give you examples of people who just won't listen. You can list a few of your own right now I bet. My strong advice is to make sure you don't become one of them.

Tom Blake, a sales executive from Columbia, South Carolina, tells about his own learning process, and about increasing his self-awareness through experience and self-reflection. "I think the thing that has held me back the most is trying to do everything. I think a big mistake that I made early on was I came into the branch organization, and there were a lot of hats I had to wear then. You just have to be the best at all of it, but I probably moved very slowly with delegating things and giving my managers and my leaders ownership. What I have uncovered is the more I give managers and the leadership in the office and even in the organization, the more I realize these people want to help us grow. And if you are willing to give those folks more ownership, you'll find people who can take it and run with it. When I have done that, that's when our office has grown. What I still struggle with today though is just trying not to do things that I know I shouldn't be doing. I should be delegating those things and giving ownership to others to do those things. When I get out of the way, we seem to move pretty quickly. So I would say that's probably the biggest challenge that I have at this point."

That's quite a courageous admission from someone higher up. But his admission alone is evidence of how much Tom has strengthened and continues to grow by looking at himself honestly. Though this is a scenario he describes at work, it really has a universal application for him beyond the office because it speaks to his learning to trust and to give up some control. It speaks to his flexibility to set aside what he thought was right and to open himself to better ways. He has the confidence to change, to admit his vulnerabilities, and to seek help, ultimately, so he can better help others.

By following Tom's example of recognizing your own fallibilities, of peeling away the layers to see where you are effective and where you are not, you too can achieve depth of character and financial rewards.

Self-Leader

Taking on this responsibility also fits into a description of leadership. In this case, self-leadership would be a good term to describe what it takes to develop an understanding of yourself. This process is marked by initiative, integrity, concentration, and courage, just as is true for other displays of leadership. Except when you are leading in public, you get the perks and accolades from those who admire you. Whereas with self-awareness, an even greater amount of fortitude is required because there is little fanfare to help buck you up. Generally the main recognition of your will to improve yourself comes from you, and privately from the people closest to you.

That's how sales phenom Lori Moncada approaches her responsibility to grow as a person. She explains, "I think it's a process. I think you learn self-leadership over the course of time. I am a person that likes to know myself as much as I can. As I'm running into situations where I might be uncomfortable, for example, I will stop and look at that to see if there's something I need to work on. I try to be as self-aware as I can, and I think that helps me in terms of how I respond to certain situations."

Whether she's interacting with clients or colleagues, she remains aware of where she is during those exchanges and senses if the conversation is going in the best direction or if it has gone astray. Then she thinks about what adjustments she can make to move the conversation to be more productive. "I feel like I encourage people to take the opportunity to be who they are and to be in that moment. I feel like that's a form of respect. If I have an employee that needs something, I'm going to expect that they're going to work their way through it with me as a resource, not necessarily have me handle a situation for them. I like them to be independent thinkers, and I try to work to their strengths." She adds, "But I won't necessarily step in and redirect them if it's outside of their personality, their wants, or their needs. So, I think the ability to recognize each person as an individual helps me."

Lori knows she is a forward thinker. An optimist. A good communicator. That she wants to make a difference in people's lives. That she wants to help in any way she can. That her integrity and being respectful are big parts of her value system. And what may come as a surprise to some, she knows that she is not competitive—not in the sense of competing with others. Instead, she competes with herself. "I won't necessarily gauge myself against anybody else. I will push myself within my own comfort zone, but I feel like there's plenty for everybody. I am very goal-oriented, but it's all personal."

And Lori knows too that she is a compassionate person. "I think it's really important to connect on as many levels with people as you can because the more you understand them, the better sense that you get of them, the more you know what's important to them. That's where you do your best work. I think that we all make decisions every second of the day. And we just have to decide to be there and do the right thing. So, yeah, I want to be there, and I want to do the right thing. I want to be available. And compassion plays into that."

She applies her self-knowledge not only to growing her success but also to lifting herself up when things aren't going well. This use of self-awareness can be particularly helpful to you when you are feeling alone on an island, without a support system in place to help you. For example, Lori describes when she first started out in straight commission sales that there were many difficult times. She had a lot of adjusting to do—to the clients, to the pressures, to the company culture. "I think what I had to do was pull myself out of it and look for all of the things that I loved about where I was at. I had to trust my instincts because my instincts told me to keep going. And I wanted to sort of speak to that. So I looked at all of the potential. That's when I started to look around. If I didn't think I was making enough money, I could see what other people were doing. I always had to see what the possibilities were. And if I could plug into the possibilities, then the rest of it didn't really matter."

So fears and pressures don't derail Lori. Instead, she looks at them as opportunities to learn about herself and applies self-development techniques to regain her usual self. Her consistency is marked by maintaining a mindset to be present emotionally in her relationships. And along with that, by reinforcing an attitude of plenty versus scarcity. "I was never the person on the phone that was very aggressive. If somebody didn't want to see me, I would spend a little bit of time trying to get them on the same page, but I wasn't overly aggressive about it. I feel like there's plenty out there. There are so many people we haven't seen. If I make dials and I can't get into a house, I have to keep making dials because there are people that are going to see me."

She applies this same confidence in trusting herself in face-to-face sales situations. She not only listens to what her prospective or existing client is saying but also to what they're not saying. "It's similar to being an athlete and having good court sense, or with the team that I have now, we call it reading the house. You want to be able to read the client so that you can work from the best place possible." Though this skill can be difficult to acquire, through increased self-awareness, you can build up your abilities to be more insightful.

In the revealing book *Just Listen: Discover the Secret to Getting Through to Absolutely Anyone* by Mark Goulston, MD, the author echoes the value of Lori's mindset. He writes, "It's easy to focus so intently on getting something from someone else—more work from a coworker, more respect from a boss, a sale from a client—that you lose sight of the fact that inside every person is a real person who's just as afraid or nervous or in need of empathy as anyone else. If you ignore that person's feelings, you'll keep hitting the same brick wall of anger, antagonism, or apathy. Make the person 'feel felt,' on the other hand, and you're likely to transform yourself from a stranger or an enemy into a friend or an ally. You'll get less attitude, less obstruction, and more support—and you'll get your message through."

At the end of day, you have to feel good about what you are doing. That's the litmus test. Ask yourself: *Have I accomplished something that helps people? Do I feel good about my interactions?*

Among all the top sales professionals and leaders I have studied and worked with, in every case their work held real meaning for them. And in some fashion their meaning was greatly derived from a sense of helping others. For example, Richard Sear, a sales executive from Wilmington, North Carolina, places a high value on helping people and making a difference in their lives. In fact, it's a central motivation for him. He's certainly no saint and openly admits that, yes, his intentions are noble, but his work still comes with disruptions and frustrations from time to time. With a good perspective gained mostly through self-reflection, though, he's learned to take philosophical approaches to those challenges. One approach is he reminds himself that the pursuit of perfection is a trap—things will never be perfect so don't worry trying to make them so. Second, he convinces himself that he will get through it. In his words, "You will; you will overcome it. You will conquer it as long as you stay focused on what the vision is and what the end result needs to be. … Just push through it and you will come out the other side stronger than you were going in." Third, after he has gotten through it, with a fresh view, he looks back and sees in hindsight that things weren't as bad as he might have made them out to be.

To create an environment conducive to this way of thinking requires that those in your circle understand how vital self-responsibility is, as well as how self-responsibility gets solidified through personal growth. Richard expresses this commitment by opening himself to candid feedback, such as when colleagues identify areas where he can grow and be more effective.

A critical point to understand about increasing your self-awareness is that it's not just an interest for today or a passing fascination to get you from here to there. It's a lifestyle, a daily commitment, a habit to be incorporated into your life to bring you to the best you can reach.

Listen to sales executive Gary Downing from Tacoma, Washington. "I evolve every day. Each day that new things are presented to me, it gives me an opportunity to reflect back on some of the training that I've had, some of the personal experiences that have made me who I am. It's an everyday journey." He says that at work he used to get so busy or focused on a task that he would get a kind of tunnel vision. Then he learned to remind himself not to get tripped up like that. He also brings to light a topic that many, no matter their position in any organization, are afraid to admit. Mostly out of fear that they will appear weak. It's human: self-doubt. Gary doubts himself at times. So what. Show me somebody who doesn't doubt themselves and I'll show you somebody with an accident waiting to happen.

Some doubt is a natural part of life. Especially if you are in a position of making decisions based on only partial information. You reach the best conclusions you can with the information you have at the time. Gary adds, "Doubt will always enter the picture and I think you just have to accept that. Don't go into a kind of denial thinking that says you shouldn't doubt, or you shouldn't question."

He also talks about other benefits that have come as a result of his increasing self-awareness. One benefit is his greater ability to see things from different points of view and better able to understand the people holding those views. Another is he is better at helping build others' confidence so they can live up to their own highest standards. And a third benefit is he is more caring.

Regional sales director Neal Quimby is another example of a leader who has applied his self-awareness directly to advancing his career. For instance, he believes the first step to moving into roles with more responsibility begins with understanding yourself. "You have to understand all you can about the mistakes that you make. You have to be real about this. And you have to check your ego at the door."

That's how he mentors. He knows firsthand that increasing his self-knowledge has been key to his promotions. For instance, it's made a real difference in his ability to manage more people as he climbed up the corporate ladder. Now he's a better communicator. Before he might have just come down on people and said, "That's fine, but this is what we're gonna' do." Today he's more inclusive and more open to discussion. In a situation where he probably would have hammered his point home, now he says something like, "Hey look, I don't think you approached this the right way, so let's see if we can work this out."

He's also better at stepping back, looking at himself, and, in his words, "being real." This is especially important for him because he already knows what he's like to work with. "I want to get in there, put my hands on the wheel, and drive the thing. So I need to just be conscious of stepping back."

His self-awareness has given him keener insights into what's most important to him as well. For instance, he didn't realize it before, but now he does: seeing people develop moves him. "There's nothing more rewarding than to sit down with an individual, teach them something, and then step back and watch them deliver it, in some cases better than I taught them. That's probably the best feeling that I could ever have. And that's why I do what I do."

Neal is highly motivated by these internal changes he senses. And that by changing himself there is a spillover effect that helps others change themselves in positive ways too. For instance, take Neal's optimism. His way of embracing challenges. His drive to win. His core principles about integrity, teamwork, bringing the best out in people, and accountability. He invested in himself and then directly applied his self-knowledge to bettering his productivity. And to bettering the balance between work and his personal life.

Sales professional Ryan Veariel reveals how his self-awareness helps him cope with success. As it turns out, his struggles are very similar to ones we all have at some point. He explains, "When I first started I had a fear of success. It was not that I held myself back, but I would find a way to return to my comfort level. I wasn't used to success that way, so I would find ways to sabotage my career so that I would feel comfortable." One of the tools he uses to manage that fear is to remind himself that he is accountable and there's no one to pass his problems along to. Next he acknowledges what barriers are holding him back, and then deals with those barriers one at a time until he is able to break through and be his usual self again.

This process of gaining self-awareness has led to some remarkable transformations in how TJ Bean (TJB), a financial advisor working on commission from Atlanta, carries himself. "I think I had a character flaw for a long time of being a little bit selfish, caring about my own personal success versus not really looking out for my client's best interests. And when I really started thinking about my value system, started thinking about where I was at in life and how I wanted to be significant, everything changed—value-wise. Now, I look at what I do every day as making a real difference."

He has another system in place to help hold himself accountable. He keeps a mental tally every day of his integrity and of his efforts to help people. TJB knows that he is prone to a pattern—just as is true for many of us—where his good intentions fall by the wayside because he doesn't carry out the necessary actions. So he's broken his process down, analyzed it step by step, to make sure he understands it is up to him. That self-responsibility starts and stops with him. This kind of discipline has translated into a distinguished career—one that is characterized by trustworthiness, a drive for excellence, and a sense of service.

"I think that the best method of accountability is how many people you see and how many people you've helped. It is not how much business you've sold, or how many contracts you've written or how much commission you've earned. I don't track average com-mission per deal but I have seen a lot of successful agents do that. I despise doing it because I just want to help as many people as possible."

What this all comes down to for TJB is that his increasing self-awareness brings with it a profound depth in how he sees his life's purpose. Simply put, he is here to help others. "A huge turn-ing point for me in my career was when my obligation to myself ended, when I no longer concerned myself with getting the bills paid, paying down debts, all the things that could be self-centered and self-focused. When everything that you desire comes from the nourishment you get from helping other people, when everything is about making sure the people you interact with really understand where they're going, when you give yourself a level of knowledge to feel confident day in and day out, when you really are making a sig-nificant impact in other people's lives, that's when a career-building path opens up for you."

Through a higher calling he answers to each day, he has found real meaning in his life. A meaning that far exceeds his own personal satisfaction, awards, or accomplishments. In short, self-knowledge is a means for TJB to express his personal values to excel, to serve, and to provide for his family.

There's another viewpoint his self-awareness has opened for him—TJB realizes he has no control over most of the changes in life. He must adapt or be left behind. With adaptation he can remain an invigorated man. Naturally, he has downturns just like all of us. Yet, he finds ways to reinvent himself, to calm his fears and anxieties, and to keep going.

For example, he describes when he went through some really low periods in his business. "I felt entirely detached, whether it be from the office, from clients, from feeling like a charge-back was coming because of something I said or something I did. It worried me to the point where those crushing failures were making me start to think, 'Is being in sales the right business for me?' It was this way because I lacked self-awareness. What that means to me is that I lacked an understanding of the importance of what I do. Joe Jordan wrote a really good book called *Living a Life of Significance.* It's about understanding how sincere business needs to be when it comes to the engagement you have with your clients, to the actual degree of commitment that you have to make to ensure success. There is no need for self-motivation and all these other things. When you get to the point that you understand how significant you are in your clients' lives, you're going to go far. It is going to become more than a career. It's a lifestyle."

This understanding led TJB to really focus on being in touch with his clients' needs. As a result he finds that his relationships with his clients have less to do with the products he offers them and more to do with the bond they share when talking about their kids, their goals, their retirements. Or when they are discussing their health now and in the future, what they are really saying is they want to make sure to maintain their dignity and their ability to make choices.

All of this brings up questions about how you can get yourself into a mindset to be as helpful and financially successful as TJB—to set aside your own fears and worries and put service to your clients first. One top sales professional I know arranges his appointments starting out with the one most likely to be successful. That way he can get a boost from the success and carry it forward. This helps him push through disappointments, which are inevitable in sales, and keep himself on track.

Another top sales professional I know readies herself every day by listening to music that inspires her and by reading quotations that are uplifting. She affirms her successfulness all during the day too as a way to help her keep going through what can be arduous work in prospecting for new clients. These affirmations help her maintain her fortitude, tenacity, sense of purpose, and joyfulness. Also, when she reaches a goal or other milestone, she rewards herself. She makes time to validate her accomplishments—maybe treating herself to a day at the spa or buying herself a new outfit. The combination of these techniques, plus her own life experience, give her a unique ability to listen to what her clients are saying—to truly take in what they are expressing emotionally and to respond with purpose and clarity.

This theme repeats itself throughout organizations where genuineness is a part of the culture. And those who adhere are rewarded with loyal clients who value being treated with respect, dignity, and honesty, equally as much as, if not more than, they value other considerations like price, availability, and convenience.

High-achieving sales professional Ryan Veariel understands that the better prepared he is, the more success he has. He relies on reading inspirational books and quotes to keep himself primed. He's got a Plan A and a Plan B and a Plan C to drive his mindset for success discipline. All of his preparation makes him more adaptable to changes and more available to opportunities. For starters, he believes in what he does. "If you believe in what you're doing, it's very easy to be passionate about overcoming any type of obstacles that are thrown your way."

This attitude was especially helpful in his first few years because, in his words, "It's very easy to get knocked off your horse, so you have to get back on it." His willpower alone, though, hasn't carried Ryan to the levels of success he has achieved. He also seeks out supportive people, ones who have a "keep going" attitude. "You have to stay in there," he says. And that means digging deep when times are tough, celebrating your wins, staying true to your values, and committing to continued growth.

Lesson Learned

An increase in self-awareness creates an increase in quality of life. At first glance this emphasis on looking inward may seem selfish. But in the most honest sense, your greater understanding of choices to develop more positive changes in yourself also puts in place fertile ground where others can grow and change themselves for the better too, just from knowing you.

Earlier, I wrote about Dr. Tanzi's work. Here is another application of his findings: As you help others, you actually strengthen the higher-functioning executive part of your brain. Your advancements are self-perpetuating, meaning, the more you grow, the more you grow. Think of it as a ripple effect with your self-knowledge making a splash in your own life, and, as nature would have it, also affecting the lives of others. One of the greatest callings you can answer is to know yourself. By changing yourself you can help spark change all around you.

Chapter 4
Build the Mindset for Success

Once you develop a greater self-awareness of regularly identifying your thoughts and emotions and how they influence your actions, the next important action is to build the right mindset. I developed a step-by-step proven model for success based on a multiyear study I conducted. I profiled, interviewed, and assessed 360 of the very best sales professionals and leaders. Currently, through my Executive Leader coaching work, I have further refined this model, which is now known as the Mindset for Success. It is evolving, as is true for life in general, and most recently includes added techniques to access the **Executive Brain**. More on this in a moment.

Partly based on some old wisdom that is finding new life again, then paired with today's groundbreaking research in psychology and neuroscience, the Mindset for Success is a blueprint that has helped many realize their highest potential. Cornerstones of this model support accomplishments while overcoming fears and strengthening self-confidence and optimism.

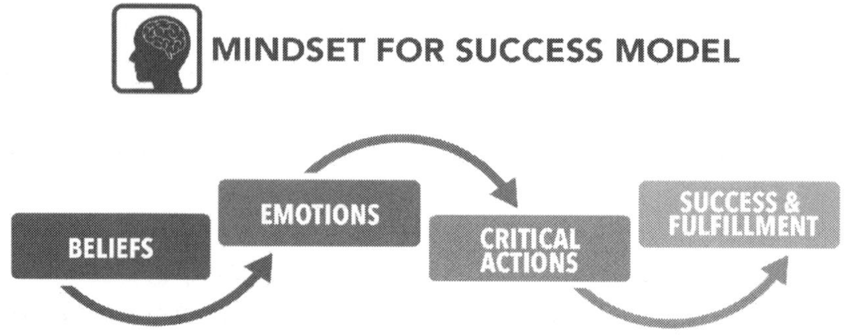

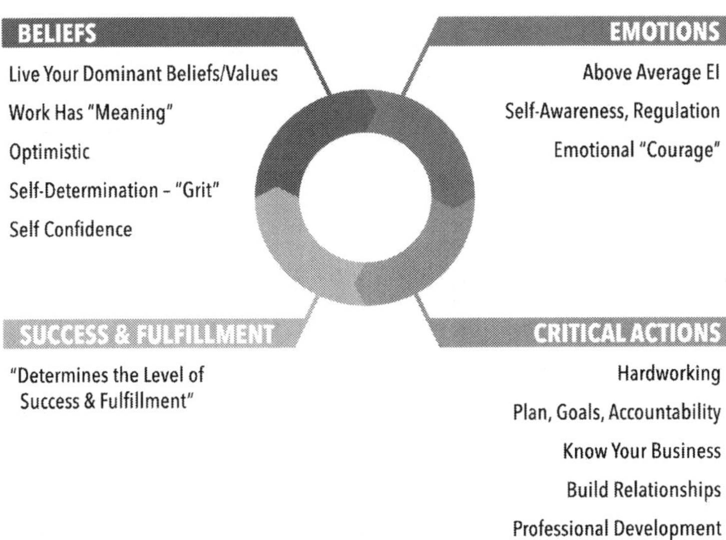

The Mindset for Success Model is based on three distinct steps.

Step 1 is understanding your beliefs. What do you stand for? What core principles guide you?

Step 2 is understanding your emotional well-being. Are you really aware of how you feel about yourself and others? Are you regularly in touch with your feelings and can you express them constructively?

Step 3 is understanding your critical actions. Do you have a good work ethic? Do you hold yourself accountable? Do you have effective relationship-building skills? Do you have a personal and professional plan?

These diagrams give an overview of the model with more explanation following:

Here's a bit of scientific background to help explain this model further. It is best to operate from the frontal lobe of the brain, often referred to as the **Executive Brain**, because that is where change occurs, both mentally and physically. Positive, innovative, and creative thinking occurs here too. And it is also where you can analyze the progress you make in improving your mindset. The Executive Brain is at the center of becoming the best you can be, and the happiest. This may at first seem too "out there," especially as it relates to your career, but I assure you it is very much a present-day topic in the most innovative organizations. In fact, companies are rushing to hire consultants to help colleagues find their "happy place" through understanding the Executive Brain.

One of the greatest advocates for this trend is Shawn Achor, the *New York Times* best-selling author of *The Happiness Advantage*. He has worked with leading businesses around the world. Here in the United States of America, his roster includes many of the Fortune 100 companies, the NFL, the Pentagon, and even the White House. Here's his take: "Research shows that when people work with a positive mindset, performance on nearly every level—productivity, creativity, engagement—improves. Yet happiness is perhaps the most misunderstood driver of performance. For one, most people believe that success precedes happiness. 'Once I get a promotion, I'll be happy,' they think. Or, 'Once I hit my sales target, I'll feel great.' But because success is a moving target—as soon as you hit your target, you raise it again—the happiness that results from success is fleeting.

"In fact, it works the other way around: People who cultivate a positive mindset perform better in the face of challenge. I call this the 'happiness advantage'—every business outcome shows improvement when the brain is positive. I've observed this effect in my role as a researcher and lecturer in 48 countries on the connection between employee happiness and success."

This sounds pretty straightforward, right? But here's the kicker—most people aren't happy and don't operate from this mindset. **Instead they live their life mostly using their least evolved cognitive functionings known as the Reptilian Brain. This lower functioning area that includes the brainstem, cerebellum, limbic**

system, and more involves going through life on automatic pilot. You react without thinking, make impulsive decisions, and, for the most part, stay stuck in what is familiar.

But there's good news. Evolution is on our side, albeit moving at a very slow pace. Over the last four million years, the Executive Brain has evolved and self-awareness has come into the fold, allowing each of us to observe what we are thinking without judgment, and through the process of increased awareness we can literally change our thoughts. So what I am suggesting is a way to enhance your own evolutionary process. With my help or without it, you're still going to evolve. But with my help, you can do it faster and more effectively.

Here's an example of how this relates to sales. Rejection goes with the job and you can't get around that. If you have a bad day, a bad week, a bad month, or one rejection after another without catching a break, then your confidence likely will take a hit. You might start doubting yourself or out of frustration break down and get a molten chocolate latte or a pint of butter pecan ice cream to try to pick yourself up. Or turn to anger and lash out or turn your anger inward and kick yourself. Sometimes you might even feel like you want to give up. These kinds of responses are typical indicators that you are operating in your Reptilian Brain.

But back to the good news. When you operate in the Executive Brain, you can handle adversity with greater success. Using the same sales example as previously where you've had a rough go, using the Executive Brain you can engage in more uplifting self-talk such as "cold-calling is challenging for everybody." Or "the service I provide is valuable so just keep at it."

Overall, being in the Executive Brain helps you build confidence and feel grateful for what you have. It also helps you maintain a commitment to the higher purpose your work serves—for example, you are not just selling an insurance policy, you are helping create peace of mind for a family's security that will also likely help their future offspring. For instance, in helping with the financial planning for a child to one day graduate with a college degree, you are part of a bridge to better quality lives for generations to come. Or your service could help ease some of the worries in a family when their loved ones get ill. At the most intimate level, you can make a difference in helping someone just get through each day knowing that you've got their back. The policy that you sell is reflecting a deeper meaning in your work, in addition to being a practical fiduciary document.

I want to be clear, though, that this Mindset for Success Model is not for everyone. It's really geared toward those who are conscientious and driven to excel, and toward those who want to contribute to making the world a better place. And frankly, these are the individuals top-tier organizations identify with and seek out. The model matches up with a culture of strong values and practicality to keep up with increasing demands for doing the right thing. It just makes good business sense.

The Three Elements in the Mindset for Success Model
1. Understanding Your Beliefs

Your core beliefs impact your emotional state, self-confidence, and level of optimism. Those core beliefs can both guide and get in the way of every aspect of your life, day and night, through your conscious and subconscious minds.

We start forming belief systems in our early years. In fact, research shows that, even in infancy, the organization of thoughts into coherent structures begins. It's no wonder then that the formative years of childhood can set the stage for a continuation of lifelong patterns for thinking and behaving. Yes, one can change as you mature and gain experience. For instance, I'm sure you can think of a number of things you used to believe in that you no longer stand behind such as "spend and don't worry about how to pay for it" that have given way to "live within your means." But the key is not just to rely on the passage of time or happening upon someone or something that brings you around to a new way of thinking. It is to rely on your self-leadership.

If only it was just that easy. Most people are not even aware of their core beliefs, let alone how they might improve their lives. So for many the idea of changing or adapting core beliefs is about as likely as flying to Mars. After all, how can you change what you don't even know exists?

Here's a broader example. Let's say that after years of hard work, you're still grinding it out but never getting ahead. It would be understandable for feelings of defeat to temporarily drift in. What I am referring to, though, are long-term, pervasive, ingrained, debilitating beliefs that have the power to chart the course of your life. A few examples of these are "I'm not good enough" or "I don't deserve success" or "The only way to get ahead is to scratch and claw my way up." Here are some other common beliefs you may not be aware of but nevertheless may still be holding you back: "My father will be mad at me if I pass him" or "I am only as good as the amount of money I bring home; any less and I am not living up to being a provider" or "I am better off laying low, flying under the radar, rather than sticking my neck out."

These harmful beliefs can come from your family, your religious affiliation, your work, your peers. And from society—advertisements, celebrity worshipping, political firestorms. In a twist of psychology, they can be further weaponized if you build them into your worldview to help you feel that you belong, are safer, not responsible, and more. For example, *I read in the news that hardly anybody has money set aside for a rainy day so I'm not going to worry about my savings. The government will come up with something. What else are they going to do, let us all go under?*

Many of these ingrained harmful beliefs are based on past injuries but still carry a sting and leave you feeling helpless at times to fend for yourself, even though in reality you are more than capable of doing so. New research is relating post-traumatic stress syndrome (PTSD), once only associated with combat troops, to psychological traumas suffered by victims of crimes or of schoolyard bullies, children of divorce, survivors of natural disasters, and more. In each of these cases, some with deeper trauma than others, the victims can be impaired when making distinctions between real past threats and the carryover to irrational, yet perceived as real, ones in the present. The result is their lower functioning part of the brain, or Reptilian Brain, decides for them.

Think of the Reptilian Brain as a recorder—it simply plays back what is in storage; it doesn't censor or alter. With the Reptilian Brain in operation, your harmful beliefs live on in the form of feeling immobilized, worrying, being mean to yourself, and procrastinating, to name a few.

However, if you are able to be aware of these reptilian stalkers sabotaging your success, then you can take steps to reframe your thinking. Here's where the Executive Brain enters the picture. For instance, if one of your colleagues is at the top in sales, rather than feeling jealous or that their success diminishes what you contribute, a healthier approach is to look to him or her as an inspiration for you to do your best. You can still strive to be number one but understand that your worth does not depend on beating others. Also setbacks are inevitable—they're growth opportunities in your long-term journey. This mindset is the difference between higher functioning thinking from your Executive Brain and lower functioning thinking from your Reptilian Brain.

Since stress can bring out a lot of the self-defeating beliefs you may be operating under, it is important to manage your tension. Allow yourself to process what you have on your mind and get some clarity on how you can build new, more constructive beliefs. Ideally, even when under stress, you will improve at redirecting yourself to healthier mindsets rather than defaulting to negative beliefs.

This brings up something I'm sure you've heard all about—the value of a positive attitude. The classic, *The Power of Positive Thinking*, by Norman Vincent Peale is one of the better known books about changing your thoughts in order to change your life. Though it was first published in 1952, current research puts some measurable data behind the author's views and shows that the brain actually morphs—that it physically changes in shape—as new, positive beliefs replace old ones. Think of the brain as having grooves that have been dug in and beliefs flow down those grooves day and night. By changing your beliefs, through self-awareness and often by repetitively training yourself to think differently, you can create new grooves. As you stop or reduce an old way of thinking, the deep grooves that those harmful thoughts have been traveling down become more shallow and eventually inactive, while the new grooves based on your healthier thoughts carve in deeper and wider.

This whole process falls within the science of brain elasticity and generally refers to the brain's ability to heal itself. At an even more basic level, it's about the Executive Brain helping the Reptilian Brain. You can accomplish this through self-questioning, self-talk, repetition of positive affirmations, visualization, and just by simply observing your thoughts, among other techniques. The applications for this science are far-reaching and offer hope to millions who suffer from cognitive disorders, such as those brought on by strokes or brain injuries, as well as from psychological conditions, including depression and anxiety.

For our purposes, we will focus on reprogramming your brain to bring out the best in your workplace performance. So let's dive in with a few questions to get you started at discovering the beliefs you operate under.

Do you see the glass as half empty or half full?

When you face a challenge, do you shy away from the discomfort or accept it as a natural part of growth?

Do you opt for the quick fix or look for lasting solutions?

Next, write down some of your own similar questions and see if they help reveal more about your beliefs. This is a private exercise that no one else needs to know about, so dig deep to find both your healthy and unhealthy beliefs. Then dissect them until you reach a central understanding of why you keep them in place. Is it because that's the way you were raised or what you were taught? Or because you evolved as a person and reached new insights? From there, break apart the harmful beliefs one at a time. Be systematic and thorough. When you've cleared enough room apart from your mental chatter, then work at ingraining new helpful beliefs to move forward with. These everyday beliefs are embedded with your more influential core beliefs.

I wrote earlier about the multiyear study I conducted with hundreds of the very best sales professionals and leaders. The following are the core beliefs that were consistently identified by these sales leaders. Please review these core beliefs as a guide for identifying your own core beliefs that are essential to your growth and success.

Core Beliefs
1. **Live by the universal guideline of "do unto others as you would have them do unto you."**
2. **Focus on service, and in some cases on fulfilling a mission, to make work meaningful beyond just earning an income.**
3. **Be optimistic.**
4. **Act with a high degree of self-determination, or "grit," and perceive setbacks as growth opportunities.**
5. **Know that feeling self-confident takes time, practice, training, and commitment.**

So how can you integrate these core beliefs into your own work daily as a sales professional or leader? Here's a story that illustrates how. Denny Riley from Cedar Falls, Iowa, started out as a struggling agent and rose to become the successful sales manager he is today. He lived the same values described above when he was out in the field and, now that he's mostly behind a desk, he continues with them and trains his sales crew to so the same. That's not to say it is easy for him. He has been really tested along the way. In fact, over the years he's had to fire friends who were agents, and even let go a family member—good people in their own right and very successful but not committed to selling with integrity and honesty. Those were gut-wrenching decisions for Denny and caused him many sleepless nights. However, he knew that based on the core values he lives by, it was the right thing to do.

Integrating more well-thought-out constructive core beliefs into your life is difficult. I won't sugarcoat it. Sure, saying or writing out affirmations can help get you started and even help you through some rough patches. Yes, you can counter the negative self-talk one sentence at a time: "I'm capable" in place of "I'm a loser" or "Stay calm" in place of "When am I going to learn to keep my big mouth shut." In fact, Dr. Tanzi is all about self-awareness and observing first, and then repetitively replacing negativity with positivity— repeatedly thinking of a positive vision, experience, or affirmation. He believes that it takes this repetition to rewire the brain.

He does, however, recognize the limitations of rote learning, as do I. My approach then is to not push but rather to guide. What I mean by that is to foster the Executive Brain to override the Reptilian Brain. Through self-awareness, understanding, and believing in yourself, you can have great, life-altering changes take hold.

Piggybacking along with the process of changing your beliefs is a process of creating higher ethical and moral standards. Overall, the two processes can give you more choices about how to feel good about your integrity and about what you give back to your clients, colleagues, family, and friends.

If you think this sounds idealistic, then you're probably right. But striving for the ideal is one piece of what can make you a better person and set you apart from those who are okay with mediocrity. Just temper your idealism with some realism because you cannot will yourself to be somebody you truly are not, but you can will yourself to be the best you are capable of.

Another step toward integrating healthier core values into your daily life is to recognize the value of depth. Pounding into your head "I'm great! I'm great! I'm great!" isn't going to make you a deeper person, but what can is a more thoughtful approach, with the knowledge that you are competent and trustworthy to handle whatever comes down the pike. That you have a strong work ethic and good intentions to be of service. That you hold a level of self-confidence without leaning on delusions of grandeur. That you recognize you are human with frailties and self-doubts, just like everyone else.

To be vulnerable is to be human. In fact, many top sales professionals and leaders attribute their success to being humble. They don't claim to be know-it-alls. Just the opposite. For example, they defer to others or at least share control of a conversation. They show respect. They know humbleness is a greater representation of power than is strong-arming. They know dominance over clients and colleagues is ignorance in today's marketplace, which is moving toward equality. In today's economy, your customers can compare prices and products without a single word from you—they may even have more information than you do. Your colleagues can google competing companies and compare salaries and opportunities, or take a big step—what used to be a big leap—to be their own boss. This parity is culling those in sales and leadership who are self-centered and controlling. And steering those remaining with the catchphrase "how can I be of service to you?"

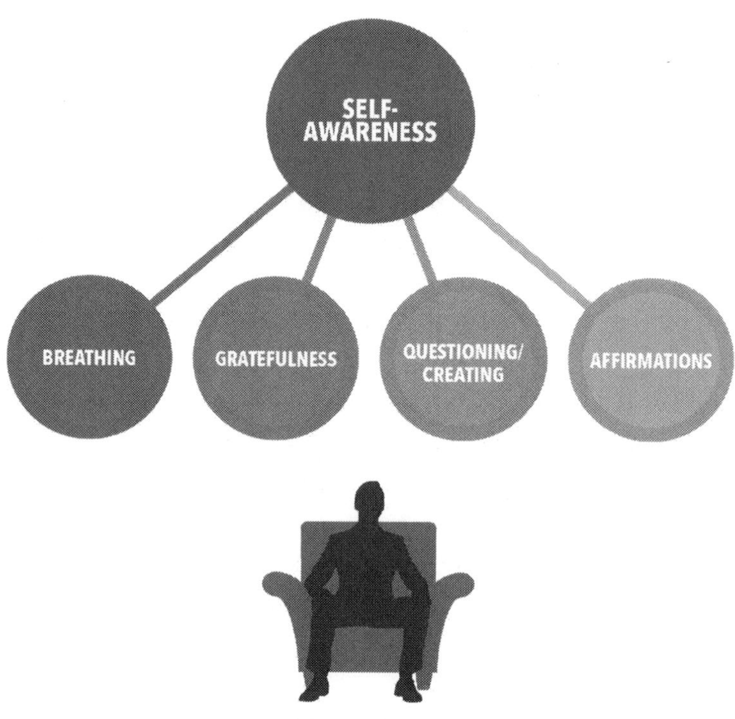

Orienting your belief system around this new dynamic so that you can stay relevant requires going beyond what's familiar and into the more proactive Executive Brain. One exercise to help you build your confidence in this new approach is to practice putting yourself in the shoes of others. Empathize with them about their fears and anxieties, then discuss how you can help bring them some comfort. And if there is good news to share, offer them your meaningful congratulations.

But there is one central element to this process, regardless of which technique you apply: your Executive Brain thrives on expressions of gratitude such as thanks for the talents you bring to the world and for the people who love you, and appreciation for the miracle of life. Being grateful will help you in just about any circumstance.

Exercise for Accessing the Executive Brain

It's okay if your thoughts wander during this exercise. That's normal. Just pick up where you left off and complete the ten steps.

1. Find a quiet place with no distractions, and sit in a comfortable position.
2. Begin by calming yourself.
3. Focus on your breathing (inhale to a count of 5; hold to a count of 5; exhale to a count of 10) and picture a pleasant scene.
4. Observe without judgment what you are thinking and feeling in the present.
5. Identify 5 things you are grateful for in life.
6. Ask yourself: *How can I be of service to others?*
7. Ask yourself: *How can I contribute to the greater good?*
8. Ask yourself: *What 3 things do I want or desire?*
9. Visualize and feel these 3 goals as already achieved.
10. Repeat positive affirmations about your specialness, uniqueness, and strengths.

To adapt this exercise to a sales call, particularly one that did not go well, add positive reinforcement through self-talk, such as

"I've been successful before. I've had many good calls and I've helped a lot of people. This negative experience is not pervasive and it's not permanent. So you know what? I'm going to have an even better call with greater sales opportunities today!"

Another exercise to help you access your Executive Brain involves emphasizing your strengths rather than dwelling on improving your shortcomings. Focusing on what you do right, on what makes you happy, and what you feel good about is part of a movement known as "positive psychology" largely brought into the mainstream by Martin Seligman, PhD. This approach maintains that what is working deserves at least as much attention, if not more, than what is not working.

We all have some tendency to fuss over our missed opportunities. Actually, there is a term for it: FOMO—Fear of Missing Out. And if you're one who takes pride in being a problem solver or being a diehard, FOMO can mess you up. The theory advanced by Dr. Seligman is that by reinforcing what you do well, you can build on your success and balance those positive attributes against your regrets. You will never be perfect—no one ever will be. So, adapting your mindset to celebrate the good, regardless of the not so good, is a healthy step forward.

With that said, feeling some negativity at times has its place because it can serve as a warning sign that a change is needed. For instance, if you feel disappointed by someone or something, channel that feeling toward changing the situation or toward accepting that you have little or no control over a different outcome.

Bringing this discussion back to sales, if a client turns you down, it doesn't necessarily mean you did something wrong. It's possible your presentation could have been smoother, but look at the experience and trust your insight. Would it have made any difference if you had been smoother? Was the customer a serious buyer or were they just picking your brain? Could it have been that their personal finances were the issue and not your pricing? Were they looking for free advice so that they could then buy online at a discount? How you view these and other challenges says a lot about your access to your Executive Brain.

2. Understanding Your Emotional Well-Being

Being in touch with your feelings is essential to mastering success in sales and in leadership. Your emotions serve as an internal radar, helping to guide you toward opportunity and away from dangers. Despite the widely known advantages of emotional intelligence, many professionals don't commit to investing the time and energy needed to achieve it.

To be honest, it is difficult so not everybody is up to it. If you were born more than twenty years ago, you may have even more difficulty because you likely were raised in a time when suppressing emotions was the way life went: nerves of steel were the norm, and all of that "touchy-feely" stuff was nonsense.

Whereas today the best-equipped are those who understand and invest in learning more about how people think and feel, and who commit to relying less on a cookie-cutter approach to communicating and instead recognize that each person responds differently to certain ways of relating. For those in leadership, they also know how to inspire others to bring out the best in them. This means going beyond the obvious carrot—money—by appealing to the deeper passions that drive each person.

Leadership often comes from an intuitive sense of being able to read others. This ability can also be intentionally developed through self-awareness. By realizing emotions are universal, that is everybody feels happiness, sadness, anger, and more, you can cultivate a sixth sense, a new language for talking with people.

To illustrate, consider this example of trying to sell to a prospective client. If you know the prospect is having a string of successes, then you have a head start in better understanding their emotional state. For instance, you likely can conclude they are feeling confident in themselves and perhaps grateful that things are going their way. Through looking deeper, you may intuit that they might also be feeling anxious about how long their success will last and fearful it might be taken away from them. Or they may feel sad or lonely if their achievements have cost them close relationships. By being tuned into your prospective client, based on what is said and even what is not said, you can adjust your sales presentation to communicate in their language.

Referring once again to the years-long study I conducted with a test group of hundreds of top sales professionals and leaders, several emotionally intelligent tendencies were common among them:

1. They scored above average in assessments of awareness of their own emotions, in their awareness of the emotions of others, in their ability to empathize, and in their social skills.
2. They demonstrated a high degree of emotional regulation, including impulse control.
3. They displayed a strong ability to have **"courageous" conversations**, including asking sensitive questions that needed to be asked, even if it risked provoking emotionally charged responses, to determine a buyer's real needs or a team member's real issues.

As I wrote earlier, part of the beauty of this Mindset for Success Model is that its benefits are universal. What I mean is that you become better at work and you become better at home with this one process. For example, being more aware of your emotions can lead to cultivating more happiness for yourself and those in your life.

If you are a sales professional, for instance, you likely have already discovered that your happiness is influential in your client relationships and the resulting commissions. If you are in a leadership position, your happiness might help justify bringing on board another administrative assistant so you have time for what you enjoy doing more of, such as long-range planning or joking around with your team. And of course you don't need anyone to tell you about the beneficial effects your happiness has on those in your personal life.

It's important here to distinguish between pleasure and happiness. Pleasure brings temporary satisfaction, while true happiness is longer lasting well-being. With true happiness, you still have ups and downs like everyone else, but there is a sustained middle ground in which you are content.

This same sense of emotional integrity can be said about sadness. By truly being with your feelings, you can gain deeper insights into your personality. Ultimately, when the sadness lifts, you will emerge as a stronger person for having weathered the hardship. It is certainly tempting to gloss over uncomfortable emotions that can come with disappointing news, but, when you do so, you shortchange yourself. By being in touch with your feelings, even the uncomfortable ones, you invite growth.

The process of understanding your emotions is a lifelong endeavor. By pursuing this course, you never stop learning about yourself because each day brings new awareness and new situations. You can feel invigorated by the challenge of learning—invigorated by pushing yourself out of a familiar rut.

If you shut yourself off from your emotional side, though, you'll likely end up more one-dimensional, resisting highs and lows to stay even-keeled. You will also increase your risk of feeling isolated, unable or unwilling to open up to those you would like to be close to out of some false sense of safety to avoid being hurt or let down. This is not about being an open book. We all need to protect ourselves, depending on the circumstances, but, as a lifestyle, it is healthier to be aware of and to express your feelings in constructive ways.

You can realize these points of view by talking about your emotions with those you trust, writing down your feelings and thoughts in a private journal, or setting aside time for introspection. Taking up a hobby or other activities elevate your mind to a highly perceptive state that best-selling author and leading psychologist Mihaly Csikszentmihalyi calls being with the "flow." There is no right or wrong way to get in the flow. It is entirely up to you to decide on which approach, or combination of approaches, works best for you. What is most important is that you commit to gaining this sense of greater self-awareness and to staying with it.

Just like most things, the more you practice being in touch with your feelings, the better you get at it. In addition, the road to understanding yourself takes self-trust and open-mindedness to unlock what is in your unconscious mind. The opposite is true as well—if you slouch off about developing more self-understanding, you will likely become rusty at it.

Now let's get back again to real world applications. For example, if you find yourself procrastinating in making a phone call to a client, perhaps underneath that resistance are emotions you don't want to confront. Typical ones could be a fear of failure or even a fear of success or feeling overwhelmed with responsibilities or feeling angry about something that has brought you to a stop.

So rather than spending days, maybe even weeks, avoiding what really needs to be done, you can apply your newfound self-awareness to get underneath what is distracting you. Maybe you realize you are avoiding calling that client because you feel impatient that they're a small account taking your time when really you want the bigger fish. By coming to this realization you can remind yourself that all clients are important, that all deserve your best service, and that all add up together to give your business viability. Or, you may decide to change your business model and target a more affluent client base. Maybe you want to make working with big fish your niche. Just think of the time, energy, and money saved by understanding that you have been resisting calling that client because you've lost your patience or because you want to focus on a different demographic.

Or maybe you come to understand that your procrastination is really about fending off worries that you might get rejected. In that case, you can tell yourself: *I've met with hundreds of clients before, and sure I've been turned down a lot. But I've still kept going.*

Taking this a step further, you can think about how feeling afraid is a part of being human. With the Mindset for Success Model, how you cope with your fears is the differential. By accepting your fears, you can understand that calming yourself down involves much more than falling back on just the typical measurements of success: power and money. Being a loving husband or wife, mother or father; being genuine and compassionate; being forgiving and generous—these, along with others qualities, are also measurements of success. Having the courage first to face your fears and second to better understand them can help you find new levels of calmness.

Whether it is through awareness of your anger so you know how to better control your temper while appropriately holding someone accountable or through awareness of your happiness so that you can more genuinely support a colleague's success, the rewards of emotional intelligence can open a new way of life for you.

3. Understanding and Taking Critical Actions

Planning and daydreaming for greatness are good first steps toward success, but when you apply those thoughts to take action for the world to see and to judge is when another level of your courage gets tested. Even if your idea hasn't yet fully taken shape, an outline can still be enough to start turning a concept into reality. The key is to take critical action.

One of the best at understanding the essence of taking action is Neal Quimby, a regional sales leader from Philadelphia. Neal has an open, questioning style that encourages his team to provide ideas and feedback. He takes time to gain their buy-in. Then he puts the plan, actions, and accountability into play. Yes, there are adjustments, but once a plan is executed, his team is aligned and moving in the same direction.

Through my signature multiyear research with hundreds of top sales professionals and leaders, along with supporting research by others, several consistent character traits have emerged when it comes to taking critical action:

1. Have an unwavering commitment to a mission.
2. Understand that having a strong work ethic is nonnegotiable.
3. Work on being knowledgeable about the products, services, and markets.

4. Know that having a plan with specific goals and actions is central to success, as is regularly reviewing and updating that plan.
5. Commit to **devoting time and resources to ongoing self-development, including relationship-building skills.**
6. Be active in career development through participation in professional organizations and other networks.

Regarding the fourth trait about having a plan with specific goals and actions, virtually all successful businesses operate with sales goals or production benchmarks. Having a target in mind and striving toward it concentrates efforts and gives a quantifiable measurement of progress.

Through my recent executive coaching work, the fourth trait has been reinforced by taking into account both professional and personal goals and lifestyles. A plan needs to include a long-term vision, values and beliefs, and long- and short-term goals that reflect a more balanced work-life perspective.

The most successful sales professionals and leaders strive for the best of both approaches—hitting their numbers while also supporting an environment that fosters integrity and caring. That's how the Mindset for Success Model operates. Built into the process are thoughtful quarterly reviews that identify the ripple effects of pursuits.

This holistic assessment translates into sustainable earnings, opportunities, accountability, and integrity. In short, think about where you want to go because, as *Alice's Adventures in Wonderland* author Lewis Carroll said, "If you don't know where you are going, any road will get you there."

I spoke with TJ Bean (TJB), the financial advisor working on commission in Atlanta who I introduced you to before, and asked about his view on goal setting for guiding his successful career. He explained that he didn't have a mission statement—instead, he had a reflective statement. "The way I have always looked at it is I have something to build up to. But I would rather kind of think about the person who is going to reflect back on the things I've done. So the way I go about my business and my life, everything, is how would thirty-year-old TJB look at the decisions that twenty-seven-year-old TJB is making? How would forty-year-old TJB look at them? When you go about it that way, you build up an accountability system to maintain your own integrity and your own kind of durability in this business."

This approach works in several other ways too. First, it gives a broader perspective on your decision making—do you think soundly or simply react? Second, it gives you a more global view on your entire life, on your priorities, on your legacy.

The Importance of Having a Personal Plan

Knowing what you want to contribute and achieve rather than just reacting to what comes your way is critical to your success. And writing it all down as a plan and reviewing it periodically—weekly, monthly, quarterly—will help you focus on the solutions and actions needed for achievement. By regularly reviewing your plans, adaptive alternatives and actions can be put into place.

Another important addition is a mentor, coach, colleague, or friend who will give honest feedback on how your plan is going and help to hold you accountable for what you have set out to achieve. From my own personal coaching experience, both as a giver and receiver, I can't emphasize enough the importance of having another genuinely concerned person(s) involved with your professional and personal plans. Their words of encouragement and of caution, and standards for self-responsibility can be game-changers, especially during your challenging times.

Exercise for Creating a Personal Plan

1. Develop a vision (or mission) statement for what professional and personal goals you want to achieve over the next three to five years; be specific about each year's goals. It's very important to state how your goals will help others. Also state

how achieving your goals add meaning, sense of purpose, personal development, and financial and material gains to your life. Creating this vision statement is an unfolding process so allow yourself as much time to reflect on it as needed. Once completed, it is much easier to update as you wish.

2. Then write down the specific actions you need to take for your vision to become a reality. Be very specific in matching actions you must take with each individual goal. If needed, go through several drafts, all the while keeping in mind how achieving your plan will help individuals, families, society, and your own financial and material needs.

3. Visualize having already successfully achieved your plan. How does it look in detail? How do you feel about it now and in the future? How do others feel about it now and in the future?

4. Affirm your vision: "I can and will get this done! It may take time, but I will succeed!" Ask yourself, *What can I specifically do today to move this forward?* Know that small steps can lead to major success.

5. Tweak your plan as needed, taking into account what is working, what is not, and what obstacles you have to overcome.

6. Let it all go emotionally and mentally. Breathe deeply—slowly inhale, hold for a moment, and then slowly exhale. Center yourself in calmness.

7. Repeat these steps each time you review your plan.

Whether you drive toward achieving specific goals or pursue an open general direction toward where you want to go, performing at your best level requires an honest appraisal of your efforts. This includes being open to fair critiques. What I discussed earlier about your belief systems and emotional intelligence ties in directly with how well you respond to this feedback.

This is a great place to introduce you to Angela Duckworth, author of the *New York Times* bestseller *Grit: The Power of Passion and Perseverance.* Dr. Duckworth is a psychologist from the University of Pennsylvania who studies what makes people successful in their careers. She has looked at many different groups. **For example, Dr. Duckworth assessed cadets at West Point during their first year to see if there were markers that could help predict which ones would successfully finish their first year; rookie teachers in tough neighborhoods to see if there were indicators about which ones would survive their first year and be effective with their students; and company sales reps to see if there were traits that could foretell which ones would stay on the job and make a lot of money.**

What Dr. Duckworth found is that it wasn't their IQ. It wasn't their talent. It wasn't their good connections. The successful ones all had what she calls "**GRIT**." They had the passion and the perseverance to look upon their life pursuits as a marathon and not as a sprint. You may want to visit AuthenticHappiness.com for a reference tool that measures your level of grit and optimism. The survey only takes about ten minutes to complete.

Right up there, according to other research, is having stamina for the long haul because slogging your way through is sometimes a part of life. Call them setbacks or learning experiences. Whatever your viewpoint is when things don't work out, know that everybody deals with their own issues—everybody. It's how you handle them that sets you apart.

So if you take an action that doesn't end up the way you wanted it to, you can pick yourself up, dust yourself off, and keep going. Or you can be paralyzed with fear, anger, and grief. Most people end up in some gray area between these two places, at least while they're trying to bounce back from big disappointments.

One way to get through this recovery process is to look at what went wrong. Often, you can learn more from what went wrong than from what has gone right. After all, some success is a matter of good timing and good luck like avocado farmers riding the wave of Mexican food and in particular guacamole's increasing popularity that I described earlier. Or you may have fortunate genetic predispositions like being athletic, science-minded, or outgoing to name a few. Simply put, many sought-after traits you were lucky enough to be born with have paved a path for you.

Setbacks can block your path. On the bright side, they can also push you to take a closer look at what you stand for and if the path that has been in front of you is still the one you want to walk along. Adversity builds character precisely because it requires you to face these complex questions (unless of course you choose to avoid them). Carol Dweck writes about this in her best-selling book, *Mindset: The New Psychology of Success.* Dr. Dweck particularly emphasizes learning from our setbacks and seeing them as temporary.

The Mindset for Success Model does too. It is an excellent tool for helping you tap into your reserves to recover. Here are the three steps simplified:

1. Understand your beliefs.
2. Understand your emotions.
3. Take critical actions.

Self-awareness once again ties directly to your career performance. In this case it applies to overcoming setbacks. The alternative of living with your eyes closed, blaming, and being consumed with hatred toward opposition, competitors, or even toward yourself only muddies your ability to take constructive action. It is this very process of moving forward despite obstacles or setbacks that will distinguish you from others who get lost in the woods.

In related studies, it is widely known that most people do not follow through on their New Year's resolutions and an increasing number no longer even bother to make them. Apparently when those good intentions to lose weight, for example, meet head-on with the real actions required to drop the pounds, no real progress is made.

If you see some of yourself in this futile cycle of having good intentions but continually falling off, try breaking up the steps of your action-taking into reasonable segments. For example, if you are a sales professional how many clients can you reasonably call on in a week? How many of these prospects can you reasonably anticipate to secure commitments from in a week? How about in two weeks?

I advise you build some flexibility into your timeline because some steps may be harder to achieve, or, as is common for many, you will likely underestimate the amount of time and work required. Your success is built on going forward, backward, and sideways. But in all of these cases, sometimes you will make progress by leaps and sometimes by just putting one foot in front of the other.

Another technique to help you accomplish what you want is to set your personal best effort as your goal. That way you can validate your success based on your integrity and not necessarily based on specific, measurable benchmarks. Later, with your confidence and focus stronger, you can add in those other measurements if would like.

And if all of this talk about goals seems like too much too soon, then you can buy some time until you are ready through a technique known as compartmentalizing—that is temporarily and consciously setting aside concerns as if they're locked away in a box where they can't distract you. To be clear, compartmentalizing is not the same as avoiding. It is more about prioritizing—you are still mindful, though the concern is in the queue waiting its turn until after you have dealt with more pressing issues. If you can hone your focus in this way, then you can achieve more of your priorities.

In support of all this, *New York Times* best-selling author and authority on leadership principles Cathy Greenberg along with her coauthor TC North wrote a remarkable book entitled *Fearless Leaders: Sharpen Your Focus—How the New Science of Mindfulness Can Help You Reclaim Your Confidence.* In their work, they emphasize four guidelines that complement the Mindset for Success Model:

1. Act with inspiring courage.
2. Respond with resilience.
3. Think from a higher consciousness.
4. Engage with a self-aware mindset.

Lesson Learned

By understanding these various approaches with their overlapping principles, you can better grasp the essentials for moving forward, even beyond where you might have believed was possible. Review each component of the Mindset for Success Model:

1. Understand your beliefs.
2. Understand your emotions.
3. Understand and take critical actions.

Within these components are techniques to access the Executive Brain, build relationships, and create plans with specific goals and actions that you can update as you wish.

As you engage with the Mindset for Success Model, you will be drawn into self-reflection. This is a normal part of the process because your increased awareness will influence your actions and those actions, in turn, will give you more to reflect on—back and forth this pendulum swings between your introversion and your extroversion. The most important point to realize is that you are responsible for both your rhythm of self-understanding and taking action.

Chapter 5
Increase Your Ability to Build Significant Relationships

You can have a great product, a great price, and even a great market. But if you don't have quality relationships with your clients and colleagues, you'll lose opportunities. More specifically, if you are a leader in an environment with little trust, you'll also find less creativity, less cooperation, and less fun. As a result, you'll face lower productivity and profitability. If you nurture trust through inspiring service, operate with consistent competency, and respect people with different viewpoints, you can lift your team to its highest potential. And from there you can build a reputation that you are good to work with, you follow through on solving complaints or issues, you are reasonable, you care, you are quick to apologize when you are at fault, and you are quick to extend congratulations when others succeed. Your rewards will come in the form of meaningful relations, loyalty, innovation, gratitude, financial gain, and more.

These people skills are important to keep in mind. Especially if you are in professional sales or leadership because most people bank on the belief that hard work will get them where they want to go. Of course a strong work ethic is important to success. It's one of the core traits of almost all highly successful people, as discussed earlier, but just one trait. Even higher up the list of traits is your character—unequivocally, it is yours to develop and express. Your depth of character can make the difference between a client signing with you or with another person, particularly when you have relatively equal prices for equal products or services.

Your character is also on bright display when you recognize that building good relationships takes effort. This largely means a commitment to finding win-win solutions to issues. Quite simply, disagreements happen. The difference between a healthy relationship and an unhealthy one, though, is how the two of you untangle those knots. In the workplace, by putting in effort to resolve differences maturely and equitably, you can, not only get over the bumpy times now, but you also set a tone for resolving the inevitable bumps to come in the future.

Top-tier leader Farshad Asl knows a lot about building a culture based on this thinking. "I truly believe open, honest communication is essential to succeed in any organization. People make it or break it, based on having or not having open communication in real time. We have different groups of people. One group of people who normally, when they're not happy, show they're disappointed and frustrated. They get angry and they hold it inside. They just shut down. Those are the ones who leave without even saying good-bye at the end of the day. A second group of people create hostile environments and start blaming others. They say, 'I didn't want this from the get-go.' A third group are people who buy in to the culture I work on building. They are constructive and say, 'This is a challenge that I need to discuss.'"

So how do you handle conflicts? Are you willing to risk some vulnerability and talk out your difficulties or do you keep it bottled up inside and stew? The first way brings you resolution and growth. It allows you to strengthen your communications, which in turn can help make your relationships even better. Naturally, in the workplace you have to discuss things in a professional manner, so this is not an invitation to open the throttle on your anger. But it is an invitation to be real with yourself and others to find reasonable solutions.

This is also true for outside the office, in your interactions with your clients. Being respectful and patient with them should be a given. But just turn on the business news and you can see the latest rant or abuse directed at a customer waiting for someone to join them at a restaurant, or one forcibly removed from a flight he or she was booked on, or millions victimized with hidden fees crammed on their phone bills. It is particularly important to be respectful and patient as the marketplace continues its transition with the "graying of America," older adults, many quite capable and intelligent in their sixties, seventies, eighties, and older, who may still need some extra care. For example, younger folks can easily access additional information from Google and social media, while older ones might need your added service to help them do this. However, building trust through respect and patience is necessary for lasting relationships with any demographic.

These principles apply across the board with all professional relationships. Keep your word. Mind your own business. Respect management's policies. Okay, on this last point, we can all admit it . . . we defer to management, but that doesn't mean they are always right. Let's be clear that there is mismanagement, just as there are mistakes made, at every level in any organization. But the truth is, at most well-run organizations, managers try to make the best decisions they can with the information they have available to them at the time—often after careful consideration and in consultation with others. Most definitely, though, they make mistakes—sometimes from poor judgment, sometimes from unfortunate timing, sometimes from choking under pressure; you name it.

Even so, I advise giving your management team high marks just for being well-intentioned. What they do is harder than it looks. If you still find yourself at odds, try to understand them. See the issue from their perspective with their pressure and responsibility to make decisions that affect a lot of people. You might just look at them differently. By working on self-awareness and being non-judgmental, you can look at managers as hardworking people too, just like yourself, with the challenges of doing the right thing. As a result, you can improve your relations with them and other colleagues, become more effective, and enjoy your work more. This requires that you invest more time in those relationships to keep them evolving as healthy alliances.

You might be thinking, *Bill, this all sounds great in a fantasy world, but it's really dog-eat-dog out there and my openness will be held against me.* Unfortunately, this is true for a lot of companies. They're either unwilling or unable to change with the times.

The good news is that, based on my research and that of others, an increasingly larger number of companies are willing and able to embrace this new business model. For instance, it is becoming more common in today's workplace to build partnerships between the leadership and those who report to them. This relatively fresh approach is replacing, or at least softening, the old-fashioned autocratic "my way or the highway." If the leadership is trying to see you as a quasi-partner and taking steps to build that kind of relationship, then treat them with the same spirit of mutual regard. Granted, at times, it may be difficult to see your boss as a partner, but you can develop a closer bond by appreciating their more even-handed approach.

Astute leaders also know that, if you plateau—if there's a sense that you're not growing—then they have a responsibility to help you reignite your career again. Together you two can strengthen your alliance and build on both of your visions. One of your main focuses in partnering is to gain an understanding of the choices you have in your career, including those to advance again and to increase your income.

There's also the reality about the work and commitment required to build these types of partner relationships. Whether you are in professional sales or in leadership, if a counterpart doesn't want to partner with you, then you have to put your energy elsewhere. For those who are onboard, though, it often is an invigorating and fulfilling experience for both people.

In fact, strong leaders feel inspired by sales professionals and teams taking on the responsibility and accountability that comes along with empowerment. An average leader always looks for followers and wants to have people who trail after him or her. But a strong leader develops others for leadership roles without having fear that "one of them is after my job."

Another big part of this partnering process is having the courage to reveal to your leader your aspirations, as well as your preferences for particular tasks. Fitting into the *Strengthsfinder* approach developed by Tom Rath, you have to be willing to say what you're best at and admit which areas you need to improve. By coming clean about your strengths and desires, if they aren't already apparent, you will be taking an important step in building a more solid relationship.

This may also mean sharing your own vision about where you think the organization should be headed, or how you would like to see it changed. A sophisticated leader will care about your views, largely because they already know that the most successful enterprises foster overlapping individuals' visions and the organization's vision. For example, to be your personal best coincides with the organization's vision to be the best in the market. Or for you to be in a position to send your kids to college coincides with the organization's vision to retain colleagues, in part, by providing them with financial security.

THE WHYS?

For those in leadership positions, communication is key in risking a traditional hierarchy model for a partnership model, and then making it work. Critical to this is communicating the "why" of an organization. According to Farshad, by talking about the "why," the "how" will get taken care of: "The piece that is missing in a lot of organizations is a lack of communication, especially a lack of communication about the why. People work really hard because they know the why. It's amazing how the whole dynamic in your organization changes when people know the why. You see everybody's 'aha' moment. 'You know what? I know why I should start doing this now. I have the buy-in. I have the commitment.'"

Here's an example of how knowing the "why" can improve performance: In financial services, you are not selling just a life insurance policy, you are providing a means for a family's legacy to continue. Clients need to plan for their futures. They need to plan for the unexpected and weigh the risks of what they can handle on their own and what they need help with to protect their future health and retirement. It is the team's role, then, to understand why the team is moved to succeed. And if money is what first comes to mind, then understand there is a way to accomplish that too because the "WHYs" sales professionals and leaders strive to meet include earning more, a drive for freedom, love for family, making a difference, being admired, or any other number of reasons.

By understanding your why and the why of others, you can tap into deeply held motivations and inspirations that fuel productivity. You don't need to be a rocket scientist to figure out that, truly, the greatest motivators are those that foster your expression of love, whether it is a love of justice, education, family, helping others, spirituality, or purpose—these intrinsic values can be tapped into through self-discovery, in particular, by accessing the **Executive Brain** discussed earlier, and then applying these motivations to your daily life.

These motivations and inspirations can also be tapped into by listening more. Through listening to others' "WHYs," you may learn more about your own. For example, preconceptions, blind spots, rigid thinking, or hardened views that have outlived their usefulness can prevent you from growing and may be escaping your awareness. Through meaningful conversations with others about their vulnerabilities and struggles, you may very well open a window to better examine your subconscious. With the resulting knowledge, you can decide whether a strong change in course or just making some minor adjustments would be best.

There's an old saying that "the only thing that is constant is change" and that is definitely true of relationships. Even if you are a sales professional or a leader who embraces the most advanced model on partnerships, from time to time conflicts are still going to come up; though they are not anything to be afraid of. In fact, conflicts and disruptions, when handled well, may jump-start more growth.

Sales professional Joe Veilleux speaks directly to this, including when he has to have serious conversations with colleagues who are genuine friends. "I don't fear conflict. A lot of people don't like it, but I like it because that's when things get done. If you're just setting things aside and letting things go, that doesn't work. So you need to hit people in between the eyes sometimes. And I'll do that."

Colleagues and clients know Joe is a standup guy. So when he has to go with "tough love," he's comfortable the other person already knows he's passionate about positively impacting their life and the lives of others in his office, family, and in his company's sponsored volunteer work. "I volunteer my time to impact the community—and I get to do that with all these employees and all their families. And when I see them at company events or if we're running a company picnic or softball game or a black-tie event, especially when the spouses and the kids are involved, I want to touch those people's lives. It's important to me. I had one of my managers say, 'I love working here.' And the kids say, 'Oh, we love it since you've been working here, Dad.' That's a big deal. That's where I get my satisfaction."

This kind of closeness also requires a mature perspective on competing with colleagues. It is, after all, an environment where everybody would like to be number one while at the same time there's a need to share information or advice to help one another. Keith Lozowski from Jacksonville, Florida, is in a leadership position. He creates an environment in his organization that emphasizes maturity about this whole internal competition thing: "It's not 'Hey, I don't want Scott to know because then Scott's going to outperform me. But more like 'I want Scott to know so that it creates opportunities for me to step my game up even higher.'"

As you open yourself and help out someone else, they're more inclined to help you when you need a hand. Also, others see your camaraderie and know you are the kind of person they want to partner with. If they see you succeeding, they'll be attracted to that positive experience. It builds from there.

So rather than seeing someone else's success as divisive, see it as bringing your team together and creating more opportunity for all in the spirit of "a rising tide lifts all boats." The positive builds on the positive so, if you think of success as available to many rather than a limited opportunity for a few, you can embrace this Mindset for Success even more. There is going to be competitive tension to some degree, but, if business is conducted with the goal of maintaining healthy relationships, you can still achieve more of your long-term vision in a team-like environment than as a lone wolf.

In addition, clients sense harmony or disharmony within an organization. Sales professionals and leaders at each other's throats send a distasteful message that the clients' needs are not as important as individual achievement in the organization. Ask RadioShack, General Electric, and Barnes & Noble, as just a few examples, about how festering internal conflicts have affected their businesses. Or visit glassdoor.com and read more firsthand insider accounts on toxic office politics that have seeped out to the public. The result is inevitably an erosion of the customer base, strategic alliances, and market share; a culture of "how can I best serve myself" steps all over "how can I best serve my customer."

Good teamwork exudes a pleasantness that attracts clients. Good teamwork demonstrates that individuals at all levels of the organization understand how to operate within a mature culture and can resolve differences for the larger good. It indicates loyalty to the organization, and clients surmise that, if a sales professional or leader is the loyal type, then they'll likely show loyalty to the client too. And it gives clients the confidence to refer other business to the organization.

Building an awareness of the importance of referrals into your basic approach is critical for Mindset for Success. Ricardo Jeremiah from Boston started out in sales just as almost all those in leadership at his insurance company do. He gives this example of how to talk to a client about referrals: "'Mrs. Jones, I want to give you my business card, and I want to, number one, thank you for the opportunity to let us come visit with you today. And the reason for my card is so you'll know who came by to visit with you. And should you want to do some additional business here, then you'll know who to contact. And with that in mind, I'm going to bring out some value to you. And if you feel you value the work that I do, I'm going to ask that you refer other people to me based on what I've done for you. Does that sound like a fair way of doing business?'

"So that's on the front end, and we teach our new agents to ask clients if they know anyone who has ever experienced any hardship being in a nursing home. And at the end of the sale, whether they got a sale or not, to ask the client if they got some value—so I think continuously talking about who you can help is important. And also, when it comes to policyholders calling the office, we teach our agents to ask for referrals at that point too. When someone has a question with their claim or if they have a question about their benefits, that's a great time to ask for referrals.

"And when an agent makes the sale out there, let's say, for example, if one of our agents sold a long-term care policy, we ask for the names of their kids. Then we'll contact their kids to let them know who we are just in the event they might have a claim against the policy, then they'll know who they're dealing with.

"Referrals are easy to get appointments with, and people that you know are easy to get too. They'll actually listen and talk with you. You're working smarter versus harder in those cases. I think early on in your career, you're working really hard because you're developing your pool of people, but then you can't continue to do your career that way. You'll just get burned out so you have to go to your warm markets."

The relationships you have with your colleagues and clients come down to the basics, just the same as in most relationships. Are you trustworthy? Do you see the connection between being trustworthy and earning the trust of others? Are you loyal? Do you mean what you say? Are you bothered when someone is disappointed in you or in the service or product you provide?

BUILDING TRUST IN RELATIONSHIPS

Sales professional Lori Moncada embraces the self-reflection needed to answer these questions. In fact, she's quite open about what makes for a successful relationship with her clients. "I approach the whole business from my heart. I want to make sure that I am working with my client on the best level that I can. And so I think that every interaction is different for me, but I do have the ability to build rapport and build those relationships with clients. And I think that's where my success stems from."

Another piece for her is that she loves her work. I wrote earlier that professionals who are happy are more productive than those who are not. Those who love their work also yield greater productivity. In Lori's case, she sees how it particularly carries over to a sense of being trustworthy: "When I'm having an interaction with somebody, I like that interaction to be as genuine as possible. So I don't necessarily try to drive an agenda. It's just a real live interaction and it goes in the direction it's supposed to go. But I don't really have a strategy so to speak. I just feel like it's important to be trustworthy, right? Be who you are; be honest."

Richard Sear, from his perspective in a leadership position, shares Lori's view about trust as an essential part of any healthy relationship. "If the people within the organization don't trust you, then you're never going to get any further." Like Lori, he knows you need to give people reasons to trust you. "I think when you display a high level of integrity and strong values with the people that you work with, to me that's where the first level of trust is going to be built. People are going to know that they can communicate with you, that you have their best intentions at heart."

He's also a big believer in being consistent with what he says and does. For him, this consistency fosters an environment for trust to build even more. For example, he believes that, if you waiver from your values or integrity, then people will doubt you. So he's solid, in his words, "not part of the time, but all of the time." Which means he intentionally makes his business relationships as personal as he can. This is special because, as you well know, the opposite approach of "it's not personal, it's business" is widespread.

Not making it personal allows for more objectivity, but it is also more dehumanizing. When your business is really about quality relationships, taking the approach of being more personal, in addition to a greater sense of service, actually becomes strategic. You forge bonds. From those bonds comes more trust. From that trust comes more collaboration. And from that collaboration comes more growth.

Richard likes to characterize this process in emotional terms: "It's important to know how the people in the organization who work with you really feel, whether you agree with them or not. I think there's some opportunity from that to also know exactly where to focus on for their growth."

This trend toward more personalization is continuing in the marketplace with even more refined tools available to better identify potential new clients and new hires, and also to better retain those already on board. Being distant and detached comes with increasing risks. Richard knows from firsthand experience in mentoring colleagues about what happens when trust gets broken and the relationship hits the rocks. "Some of them take it personally. I see them from time to time not investing as much in the relationship piece. When they go through a phase like that, at some point, they realize they've been hurt. Sure, you're going to be let down at times. But you can't stop believing in people because the minute you do that, you're not going to be moving forward." So he asks them "Can you fight off the cynicism? Can you get back to being genuine and connected for new relationships?"

Sales manager Chris Lewis from Dallas sums up the challenge this way: "You have to be willing to put yourself out there. You have to be willing to sometimes overlook mistakes. You have to find people that are willing to overlook your mistakes."

The one area, though, where he has a zero-tolerance policy is with lapses in integrity. "We take that very seriously. It's just not worth it to have somebody running loose. And, if you're going to be out there and you're going to have our jersey on, we can't have you doing things that are unfair, improper, or whatever you want to label it."

Sales executive Gary Downing adds to the practicality of building trusting relationships: "Here's the thing about trust in my opinion. A lack of trust slows everything down because you're not focused on the end game—you're focused on the minutia that gets caught up. If you have a trusting relationship, you're focused on the objective at hand, and you don't get tripped up along the way. You don't doubt. You don't question motives."

Nate Richardson, a senior vice president from Parsippany, New Jersey, resonates with this link between success and building trust in relationships. He has peace of mind that people trust and believe in him. He finds they're more willing to listen to and take to heart what he says. These rewards constantly remind him to make a conscious effort, in between all of the meetings and reports in his demanding schedule, to build these meaningful relationships. As he sees it, to do otherwise is to invite trouble.

Those who work with Nate know the priority he places on keeping relationships growing. For him, that comes down to integrity. Or in his own straightforward words "doing things the right way."

"We talk a lot about selling to our clients like you'd sell to your grandparents—about doing the same thing in either situation. So we always want people to be focused on doing business the right way. Doing right by people and if they do that and they go out and sell based on clients' needs, and deliver on those needs, then we're going to have very few problems."

Neal Quimby seconds that sentiment: "If you say you're going to do something, you have to do it, with no smoke and mirrors. You have to just let people know the whole deal. Even though they might not be able to handle the information, to build that trust, you have to be open with them and you have to be honest with them."

Of course, not every relationship is going to work. You may find that you are just not compatible with a client or colleague. In these cases, fall back on a candid conversation and try to iron out your differences. Perhaps getting things out in the open can prove to be a growing experience for both of you. Or it may be that you simply gain a better understanding of your differences and can "agree to disagree." In these situations, it can be helpful to talk with someone else you trust before confronting the person you are having difficulty with. That's because you might unconsciously be bringing in your own biases and judgments, or your own agenda to be right, when really what is most important is gaining a better understanding of the troubled relationship. You essentially want this conversation to be neutral and not highly emotionally charged.

Courageous Conversations

It takes courage to confront the other person in a difficult relationship. But by doing so, you seize an opportunity to learn and hopefully improve the situation. You also demonstrate your priorities. You show yourself to be a caring person and genuinely interested in a resolution, which typically means having the ability to unearth the root cause of the conflict and then find common ground on which to reach an agreement.

Despite my encouragement to face difficult conversations, many of you will still avoid them. If you are among the avoiders, then I ask that you please think more deeply about your avoidance and consider meeting halfway. For example, ask the person some questions to try to get a better understanding. And leave it at that. Don't reveal your feelings. Don't drill down to what you think the problem is. Just ingest their answers and move on. The benefits of at least trying something, no matter how small, as a contribution toward resolving the conflict often outweigh the long-term consequences from glossing over it. If, however, you are ready for a fuller conversation, there are some specific tools you will likely find helpful.

First, **be respectful**. Recognize that each person comes with their own set of values and trials that influence their thoughts and actions. Understanding those characteristics can help you find more middle ground on which to build a dialogue. Second, seek a **mutual understanding** that there is a solution somewhere, somehow. Granted, it may not be the most desirable one for you, but there is a way to mediate the differences. Third, keep the **discussion civil**. If you have valid criticisms, express them constructively. Fourth, **pay attention to the tone and direction** of the conversation. If it escalates, be the first to take the high road and calm the emotional intensity. Listen rather than react. And last, **strive for an action plan**. Decide what steps are going to be taken to prevent the disagreement from recurring or from getting worse. According to the book *Crucial Conversations: Tools for Talking When Stakes Are High* by Kerry Patterson, et.al, setting an action plan creates a culture for accountability where progress can be measured and adjustments can be made as needed. *Crucial Conversations* is an excellent resource with practical tips and exercises for handling difficult relationships.

It's important to understand too that being proactive is invaluable to reduce breakdowns in communication. The most successful sales professionals are masters at this. Every single aspect of their business is based on relationships. Everything they do is based on how many relationships they nourish.

To have this kind of discipline requires a willingness to get close to people. As it relates to clients, you have to keep a level head to objectively guide them, but you also have to recognize the naturally occurring personal attachment that comes from such closeness.

I wrote earlier about TJ Bean. He tells it this way: "It's amazing when you're in a person's home and you have taken the relationship from the surface level to really kind of digging deep into their goals, their children's goals, and into how much you know about their grandchildren, how much you know about someone in their family trying to buy their first home. When you really dig in and people start crying in front of you about their lack of planning, their lack of preparation, and especially when they start talking about the hopelessness they feel their grandchildren struggle with in building a life, that is when you can get into a great conversation about the power they still do have—whether or not they are healthy or financially savvy.

"The power that they still have is an ability to make a significant impact on their lives through financial planning and through all the other resources available to them. We can empower them and that's where the benefit of my service really comes to mind for me."

Another top sales professional traces his commitment to building relationships with clients to the values his father taught him. Call it "old school" if you want, but what's old is new again in today's market. He views sales as servicing clients by understanding their needs and committing to meeting those needs. And he views the best relationships as the ones that withstand the test of time. Then there's one other word that stands out to him: care. He genuinely cares about his clients. Genuinely understands that those relationships mean everything to his life's work. To treat clients otherwise would leave him feeling uncomfortable because this is just a part of his personality. He can't turn on and off his care for his clients.

Holding yourself to this higher standard—being sincere, trustworthy, and committed to doing the right thing—takes a true Mindset for Success. This is the case for the seasoned pro as well as for the rookie. As an example, there was one newbie who fell into her career with no prior sales experience. Yet, she has risen steadily in large part due to what she describes as being a people person. "I genuinely like the people that I'm sitting down with. I look at every person on a sales call as my grandparent or my parent. How would I want someone sitting down with my parents to treat them? And then I use that to make sure that I'm respectful but knowledgeable and professional. And it's out of this respect for my clients' trust and faith that I walk the walk. I don't just talk the talk. That has allowed me to experience the success that I have."

"By just being human" is the straightforward answer to the question of how she largely builds this connection. By relating to the same struggles and vulnerabilities as her clients. By being down-to-earth. By being genuinely caring. By treating people the way she wants to be treated. By doing what she says she's going to do—and in her view on this point, "promise less if there's a chance you think you can't deliver in full." She too sees building a level of trust as vital, not only to the client in front of her, but to future clients: namely, through referrals from those who know she is a professional who can be trusted with their extended family and friends.

Highly successful insurance agent Mindy Klarman from Morristown, New Jersey, views her role in serving clients more as a partner rather than a persuader. "I'm not a pushy person. I will explain everything that needs to be explained and if it's not something that they're ready to purchase, then I just leave them my card. I let them know that I'm available when they're ready."

She also reveals personal information about her own financial planning to "level the playing field" in the relationship—meaning not being controlling or judgmental with her clients—and to show she personally invests in the services and products she represents. She believes this adds to her credibility and essentially says to them that she understands what it's like to be on their side of the table. "I share that information with them because I know what it's like to be in a situation of needing care and not having coverage."

To truly embrace these views means upholding your values in all areas of your life. This is about a way of being, a lifestyle choice to engage in relationships with honesty and trustworthiness as a necessary part to live up to your fullest potential. Certainly there will be those who have no interest in the Mindset for Success Model yet will still outperform you. Maybe they are more skilled, more experienced, more connected, or more lucky. There are always exceptions to the rule—the chain-smoker who lives to be ninety-five, the college dropout who makes billions, the sales representative who gets in and out for a quick sale without putting in time or energy. They've all beaten long odds. But how about you? Do you want long odds or do you want the odds in your favor?

Lesson Learned

Greater self-awareness is a pivotal factor in the level of success and fulfillment you experience in your life. In addition, knowing your own "WHYs" and those of your organization are at the heart of what gives real meaning to your work.

Key elements of the Mindset for Success Model form the foundation for building and developing quality relationships. Essentially that foundation centers on "do unto others as you would have them do unto you." And the ability to, and belief in, having "Courageous Conversations" contribute to building trust in significant relationships. These are all skills that can be learned and developed with practice.

Chapter 6
Crack Open the Secrets
to Great Sales

As a sales professional putting yourself out there every day, trying to serve existing clients and to find new ones, you need a healthy mindset just to keep up the rigorous pace. For instance, there is no time to beat yourself up over setbacks. You have to accept, learn, and move on, which is often much easier said than done. That's why more sales professionals are seeking additional support. As I wrote earlier, increasing your self-awareness is the first step to bringing you more in sync with your clients and connecting on a more personal level.

First, let me say that I know it takes a certain inner strength to succeed in sales. Period. That is a stand-alone from all of the strategies, models, and support staff available to you. Professional sales requires you to rely on yourself and your inner foundation to survive, and then to flourish. This inner strength, this self-belief, can be developed like a skill through self-awareness, thought regulation, and practice.

When you are out there on your own, for instance, sitting at the kitchen table across from a prospective client and talking with them about real estate, supplemental life insurance, home remodeling, or other investments, there is always one consideration that carries across all of these conversations. And that is you need to have an intuitive sense of your client and of their situation.

For example, it's quite likely they are at least a bit nervous. They might be worried about the costs you are going to lay out. Or they might feel uncomfortable in revealing personal information about themselves and their family, maybe embarrassed about how to come up with a down payment, or how they've never really planned for retirement.

In consideration of this very common experience, I strongly suggest right from the start you express **that you are grateful for the opportunity to talk with them about their private matters**. For instance, your opening can go something along the lines of "thank you for your time to talk with me." Regardless of anything else, thank them right away. That's how you start. Being appreciative takes you to the Executive Brain where creativity, opportunities, and solutions are found.

Also, recognize it is both a compliment to you that you have earned their trust enough to even get this confidential conversation and a compliment to you that they see you as offering a service worth the personal discomfort to have a conversation. If you haven't already met those two criteria, then they won't even take the time to invite you in. So recognize the respect that is shown to you, even before you meet, and put this thought "in the bank" to help build on your sense of service.

Next, have a plan in mind about your presentation. Maybe it's your style to lead off with demonstrating a sense of your expertise. Or maybe you like to rely on what feels natural and spontaneous in the moment. Or it could be that your plan is to mostly listen and ask open-ended questions so they do most of the talking.

Asking open-ended questions and listening to the answers is the best sales approach. By continuing with reflective questions, you can uncover the real needs of the client, help them acknowledge those needs if they are not already apparent, and then help guide the conversation toward identifying solutions.

Regardless of which of approach is the most comfortable, each approach requires first having a solid understanding of what goes into a formal presentation—though one that you adapt in the moment and present as sincere. Generally speaking, rehearsed scripts that come off as "canned" do not get results as good as those that are free-flowing, genuine, and responsive to the client's needs.

You are required to discuss disclosure statements and contracts, but, even in those driest of discussions, you can build your relationship with patience and understanding. As Daniel Pink advises in *To Sell Is Human,* have real conversations to help the other person. If you don't know something or need more information, that's okay too. Just use those times as opportunities to demonstrate your sincere concern by getting back to the client with the answers and to establish your reliability.

Here are some key steps you can apply to improve your conversational skills:

1. **Be genuine in connecting with the other person.** Be open and receptive. Show empathy and be aware of your thoughts, such as ones based on judgments that might inhibit your greater sense of being of service.

2. **Be sure your attention is on what the other person is saying and not on what you plan to respond with next.** What the person says may affect you, so resist knee-jerk reactions, and, instead, stay focused on being present, calm, and observant.

3. **Question, question, question.** Ask questions. Their answers can give you more in-depth information that the person might not reveal on their own. Ask, "Is this the point you're making? How did you come to this conclusion? How do you feel about things? How can I help you?" Asking questions is the foundation for establishing a real and genuine connection with the other person.

4. **Make eye contact and have receptive body language.** Be aware of what the other person is nonverbally communicating. Have a compatible tone of voice. Pause after you speak to give them room to talk, and then validate what they have said.

5. Be aware of **Neural Resonance**; neurological studies have shown that when two people's brains are activity engaged and mirroring each other, normal brain defense barriers are broken down and each of their brains becomes more open and trusting. The CASA Model Techniques are designed to help you achieve a state of Neural Resonance in sales and leadership. Your words, pace, and tone, plus your body language, can subconsciously open the other person's receptivity to feel your care, empathy, and desire to help them.

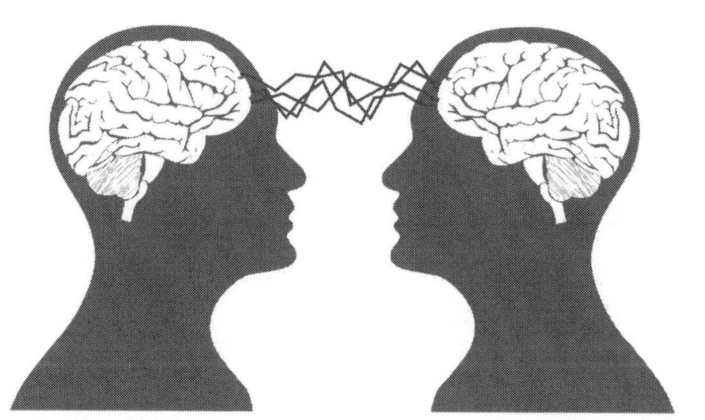

When you listen well, you also appreciate more deeply that you both are working on solutions to meet the client's needs that will better their life in some way. That supplemental health insurance is not only reliable coverage, it's also a safety net for their family. It's freedom from worrying. It puts in place some comfort for a time when your client or their loved ones might face major life transitions. And with life insurance, it's not only a solid investment in your client's financial portfolio, it's also an expression of their love for those closest to them. It's a declaration about carrying forward the values, morals, and principles they live by.

Another part of your deeper connection is that you are an expert on your product or service. This increases the client's confidence in you, as well as your own self-confidence, and raises the likelihood of your success. It also saves you time in troubleshooting should a problem arise and helps to keep you from overpromising what you can deliver.

So we have come back full circle to understanding that professional selling rises and falls on how much you understand yourself. For instance, how you manage stress, rejection, and hope. And how even-keeled you can stay about what is in your control and what is out of your control because there are rarely occasions where everything lines up exactly to your liking. In fact, sometimes "good enough" is "good enough."

There is a quote by eighteenth century French philosopher Voltaire that is often cited by sales and leadership consultants, "Don't let the perfect be the enemy of the good." You can attain your goals without having to attain perfection. By helping your clients realize the same, you can help to ease their tension and fear about making mistakes in their decisions and instead help them to focus on the practical benefits that can result simply by making a reasonable analysis. To keep pushing for perfection can just be a mask for procrastination.

For example, with your sales presentation, ask yourself if you know it well enough to do a good job. Seize the opportunities available now and simultaneously keep working toward more excellence, rather than waiting until you have some illusion of perfection.

Also, focus on feeling confident in your ability to handle any situation, even if you don't have all the information. It's okay. We're all imperfect. Plus, getting back to your client with that information is an opportunity to show your commitment to being of service to them.

And I wrote earlier, the Mindset for Success Model's foundation includes the basic principle of treating others the way you would want to be treated. For example, do you like being pressured? Probably not. And your clients don't either. They also do not appreciate fear tactics. And they do not appreciate arbitrary deadlines to squeeze in a decision. So rather than coercing, try informing and offering guidance while knowing in today's marketplace, you are only one of several providers of information along with the internet, friends, colleagues, *Consumer Reports,* and so many other outlets rounding out their view.

Risking credibility by shaving corners or overpromising will likely catch up to you. So will forcing a sale. If you are meeting a client who is vulnerable, perhaps they're elderly or otherwise unable to do their due diligence themselves, they are at a higher risk of being taken advantage of—chances are, you or someone you have heard about has been in this position. With an emphasis on doing right by your client, it may be that you lose out on a sale, but it is better to take the high road than to go in for the kill. It is better to hold your integrity as a treasure; guard well your reputation as a person to be trusted.

You'll notice that what I am talking about here has more to do with strength of character and less to do with sales strategies such as overcoming objections or up-selling. That's because in order to have a sustainable business, you have to build on your relationships. People don't buy from you just because they want your product or service. They buy because they feel comfortable with you. You yourself have probably chosen to go with a particular provider because they felt right to you, even though less expensive or different options were available elsewhere. When your provider invested themselves in the relationship with you and you reciprocated, a bond formed that carried more value than just the commercial interaction.

I have already cited research to corroborate this and don't think you need any more evidence for what you already know to be true. You know, based on your own personal experience, that people are generally more responsive when you engage with them emphasizing sincerity, quality of relationships, and service. By following this formula, your own happiness grows. That then carries forward to your other interactions and the cycle keeps repeating itself.

So there really is no trick to being good at sales. Mostly, it is about being genuine. Letting your self shine through, along with being knowledgeable and accountable. The internet alone makes it too improbable to compete on price. **The "X-factor" is you. You**

are the differential in how well you engage with your clients to best meet their needs and to be of service when they need you.

This distinction goes beyond building a connection between you and your client. It also extends to your organization's entire client base. You are a part of a community; one with your service on the front line, coupled with the administrative assistants in branches and the senior management at headquarters. And just like most communities, the more you and your colleagues come together, the more your community grows.

Ryan Veariel exemplifies this insistence on building only quality structures on top of solid foundations. "When a client gets sick, they come to you for help to make sure that their claims are paid. If they then have long-term care, they go from the hospital into a nursing facility—you're still there to protect them. If they then pass, we have the availability to make sure that their loved ones can be taken care of without having to go through 1-800 claims and things of that nature. So from sick to passing on, I'm there."

Overall, he refers to a personal philosophy that keeps his priorities straight about the importance of exceeding customer satisfaction. "'Go the extra mile because less competition is there.' If you want to do what's right for your client, then obviously they're going to want to stay with you. Going above and beyond allows them to see the value, not just in the sales transaction, but also in the way you are there as an extension of their family. They see that you're a person who cares about them. I try to do that every time. It's the core of my business."

And in the event some dissatisfaction arises, Ryan addresses the issue immediately. "You need to go above and beyond to make sure that whether it takes a phone call or a personal visit involving agent care or your manager, you will do whatever is needed to make sure that it's resolved immediately."

TJ Bean also displays a work ethic and commitment to excellence. He draws a lot of his strength from role models such as his grandmother. He describes her as having an abundance of inner peace and showing no sign of frustration or sense of hopelessness.

Instead, her love for life and zeal to continue, even in the face of strong adversity, helps lift him up. TJB takes that inspiration with him wherever he goes.

When TJB first reaches out to a prospective client, it isn't about selling; it is about building the relationship. Then after an annuity or policy is established, the foundation they already built together foretells the deep level of service that he will follow through with. "When I start going in and doing the work, seeing the situations they're in, like dealing with the relatives who are now caregivers, the spouses who have been put in a really difficult position of now having to quit work early, or the children who have had to quit work and move in with their parents—that gives me an entirely different perspective on how important my career really is.

"Because at that point, I no longer think about things like commission. I start thinking about the here and now and what I can really do to affect change. What actions I can take in people's households to make sure that they have peace of mind going forward."

TJB approaches each client thinking that he is going to be there for them throughout their lives. In that sense, his marketing efforts are ongoing. "It started with the way I initially positioned myself when I met somebody. A lot of people asked me questions, and in my mind, I answered them while thinking to myself, 'How can I position myself to make sure I am going to be in your life for the next five years, ten years, or twenty years and that I am going to be in your children's lives?' So I soon changed over to always marketing myself for a long-term position."

He goes on to further describe how he views his client relationship. "I really look at my belief system as something that's at the core of what I share with every client. The way that I start all my relationships is I ask a simple question. I say, 'When I come back in five years, do you think the things that we have discussed today will still be a priority, will they still be important to you?' And when they say things like, 'I have no idea what you mean about the insurance decisions that we are making.' I answer, 'You are going to keep this insurance long after you purchase it today, long after the next three or four years. This is insurance for your legacy.' When I start saying things like that, I get into a deeper conversation with the client. They come to realize that this is going to make an impact on their children, grandchildren, and great-grandchildren that is far greater than they probably thought of."

By approaching his work in this way, he underscores his central commitment to engaging with the person, to being of service to them, to understanding them. Part of his confidence to engage comes from knowing what he is talking about. He can back up his recommendations with sound reasoning based on a substantial depth of knowledge. This fits in with his overriding focus to be of service.

On the question of whether he closes a sale or confirms a sale, as you might imagine, TJB registers on the side of confirming. "When you close a sale, you are literally putting a person in a situation in which they feel obligated to say yes. *But when you confirm a sale,* they've already made a reasonable and emotional decision toward saying yes, toward why they're saying yes—and they understand even after you leave why it's going to bring them peace of mind to have that product. And peace of mind to have you as a resource."

In terms of closing or confirming sales, a top sales professional in property management also characterizes himself as the confirming type. He sees his role as educating clients—explaining possible solutions rather than trying to sell one to them. A part of his approach is listening to concerns and then looking deeper to better understand what is really beneath them. For instance, if the wife says, "My husband isn't much of a handyman," he thinks she's probably asking about maintenance costs for their rental property. In establishing this kind of relationship, the process of being of service progresses naturally. From there, he works to exceed customer expectations, which often leads to greater customer loyalty and referrals. Leading with excellent customer service remains a cornerstone of his success.

There is a strong point to be made here about "confirming a sale" versus "closing a sale." The initial step in the sales process is about "sitting down" versus "driving through." Sitting down is all about talking, connecting, and building a relationship versus the driving through, which, as the phrase implies, is like a fast-food order with a quick transaction ending with a close while the car is still running.

Today's increasingly knowledgeable consumers know when they are being treated like a drive-through and they don't much like it. They know quite well that you want their additional business and referrals, and to get those you have to sit down with them. They want you to be of service in helping them identify their needs and confirm their decisions about solutions that will meet those needs.

The CASA Model

There are some specific techniques for connecting more effectively and for building more accountability into relationships by using an important submodel named **CASA**. **CASA** is an acronym for

Connecting on a genuine level with oneself and others
Agreement on what goals and actions are to be achieved
Skills centered on self-awareness, self-regulation, and listening
Accountability for ownership of goals and actions to be achieved

There are three distinct CASA Techniques: I) Connecting and Selling to Others; II) Connecting as a Leader for Coaching and Accountability; and III) Building Stronger Relationships Through Self-Awareness, Trust, and Listening Skills.

CASA I Technique—Connecting and Selling to Others

Begin with these three principles that will shape the more detailed exercises to follow:

1. Determine the value of your investment in greater self-awareness and relationship-building skills.
2. Reflect on, and then integrate into your belief system, your mission to genuinely partner with your prospective and existing clients to find solutions to their needs.

3. Remind yourself that fears and anxieties are a normal part of the sales process and that, by managing feelings, you can transition to the success-oriented Executive Brain.

Next, apply the following phases of the **CASA I Technique—Connecting and Selling to Others** to help guide you through the complete sales process. With discipline and practice, this technique can serve as a resource to help keep you on track and, if you get scuttled, to help get you back on track.

A. **Before meeting your prospective or existing client**, go over the following points. Feel free to write down your thoughts, knowing that this is for your own private use and nobody else needs to see your notes:

1. Ask yourself, "How do I feel about this meeting with my prospective or existing client? What are the positive and negative thoughts or feelings I'm experiencing?"
2. To reinforce the positive and address the negative, ask yourself, "Am I on a mission to really help this person? Does my service or product help to meet their needs?"
3. Affirm, "I am the differential! I am the added value! My dedication, service, and attitude are special and unique! It's okay to make an innocent mistake and not have all of the answers. I know that setbacks, challenges, and fears are a natural part of life and are learning experiences."
4. Ask yourself, "Am I prepared for this meeting? Do I know my products, services, and market information well enough?"
5. Move to a quiet place and focus on your breathing. Get calm and centered. Visualize yourself building a strong relationship with your prospective or existing client. See it in detail. Feel it. Enjoy it. Celebrate it.
6. Now turn your attention to better understanding your prospective or existing client. Anticipate their concerns. Imagine yourself in their shoes, wondering what kind of

person you are. Be aware that "you" are the real purchase they are considering. So imagine them asking themselves, "Do I like you? Do we have some things in common? Can I work with you? Are you just trying to sell me something to make money? Do you really care about me—about my wants and needs? Can I trust you to be there when I or my family needs help?"

B. **At the sales meeting** with your prospective or existing client, understand that you are mostly improvising from the moment you knock on their door, no matter how much you have prepared. You can't anticipate every problem, be compatible with every personality type, or handle every rejection. The following exercises—by either applying just one, a few in combination, or all four—can help you stay composed:

1. Say to yourself, "It's okay. My self-awareness, beliefs, and sense of mission will get me through. I am becoming more comfortable facing the unknown."

2. Say to yourself, "Relax, smile slightly, and keep my absolute belief that I am here to help. I am aware of their verbal and nonverbal communications."

3. Say to yourself, "I am a good listener. Being a good listener is pivotal to my connecting and to my success." After an appropriate amount of listening, ask thoughtful questions. "Is this your concern? How do you feel about this product, service, or recommendation? How can I be of service to you?" Be aware that your best questions can help lead them to make a decision about whether or not to buy what you are offering. Maintain your integrity by affirming, "The possible solutions must be in their best interest. The more they recognize it is their decision, the better our relationship will be."

4. Say to yourself, "It's okay if I don't know the answers to all of their questions right now. It's not realistic to expect that. But I'll definitely get back to them promptly with the needed

information. It is an opportunity for me to demonstrate my quality of service.

C. **After you have met** with your prospective or existing client, make an assessment:

1. Ask yourself, "Did I achieve my goal? What went right? What needs work? What changes do I need to make for greater success?"
2. Reaffirm, "My overriding mission is to be of service."
3. Send a thank-you note to your prospective or existing client and reaffirm, "I am committed to taking other relationship-building actions."
4. Reaffirm, "My Mindset for Success is a proven model for bringing me the results I want and deserve, starting right now with my next call."

D. **In the event your meeting did not go well** and you are feeling down, you can add the following exercise to both address and overcome a negative mindset.

Ask yourself and answer:

1. "Is this permanent? No."
2. "Is this pervasive? No."
3. "Is this personal? No."

Next, to transition to accessing your Executive Brain, ask yourself and answer:

1. "Have I felt well connected on other sales calls? Yes, I get compliments all the time about how caring and patient I am."
2. "Have I had successful calls before? Yes, plenty of them and for even much larger sales."
3. "Can I have even more successful calls? Yes, definitely! I am ready now for my next call."

4. Reaffirm, "My overriding mission is to be of service."

5. Reaffirm, "I am committed to taking other relationship-building actions."

6. Reaffirm, "My Mindset for Success is a proven model for bringing me the results I want and deserve, starting right now with my next call."

Lesson Learned

The models and techniques identified in this chapter are proven keys to greater success in sales. Make them your own. Integrate them into your sales preparation and into your daily routine.

You truly are the differential in any sales call. Your sense of being on a mission to help, provide service, be there in time of need, and be genuinely caring are factors that are in your control while so many other factors are not. Certainly you need to have a competent understanding of your product, but you don't need have to have all the answers all the time. Your core beliefs take precedence.

The CASA model techniques for connecting and accountability—especially those applied after a disappointing sales call to help restore your Executive Brain functions—are rock solid.

Chapter 7
Leadership Starts with You

You don't need a title to show you're a leader. In fact, anyone can be a leader, really anyone who takes the initiative and has the insight to carry themselves as an inspiration to others can be. A parent doing their best to bring up his or her kids to be respectful and thoughtful or a sales professional showing self-restraint not to oversell, particularly when the client is vulnerable and dependent on guidance, are both examples of leadership. As is a person fighting cancer or other personal hardship with courage and grace. The principles are generally the same when you speak of business leadership in terms of an individual's ability to be decisive under pressure, mobilize an organization toward a common goal, and empower others.

Leadership starts with you. What I mean is self-leadership is defined by your integrity, mental and emotional discipline to maintain a Mindset for Success, willingness to confront the unknown, and so many other traits that add up to your overall character, which then get applied in a larger context, like in your career.

The main reason why I have tied leadership to selling in this book is that these two areas are becoming more closely linked. This linkage is driven by the impact of technology and the result is that just about everyone now has access to enormous amounts of information that used to be exclusive to only business leadership. Today a leader's essential skill set must include more of those of a sales professional: an ability to influence and persuade others to change, take action, or reach agreement.

In response to this evolution I have developed a model for effective leadership that takes into account two essential traits—one is the ability to build relationships, and the other is the ability to remain accountable and hold others accountable.

In the diagram below, the relationship vector refers to your ability to connect with others at a meaningful level—a connection that speaks to mutual trust, respect, and understanding. It requires that you let go of any pretentious display of authority over your colleagues and reveal yourself as a person they can relate to—one who has highs, as well as lows. It is also characterized by being light, accepting, and embracing of some sense of equality among all.

LEADERSHIP MODEL

Accountability is what you already know it to be. It is an integral part of effective leadership (and of everyday life), yet it can be surprisingly difficult to establish—so many people would rather blame or make excuses. Much of their denial of self-responsibility is an attempt to stay clear of the consequences for things that do not work out in fear that they'll be fired, demoted, iced out, ridiculed. Ironically, it is precisely during those times when accountability offers the greatest opportunities to forge your place as a strong leader.

Stepping up and taking responsibility can also help create a culture where others do the same. As Drs. Greenberg and North write in *Fearless Leaders,* "It takes strength and fortitude to admit to a mistake. There's nothing easy about it. You have to fight every natural impulse to allow yourself to be open to ridicule or judgment. It's an enormous sign of power to those around you when you can show them that you're not afraid to fail or admit to having responsibility for what's not working."

This brings us to the **CASA II Technique—Connecting as a Leader for Coaching and Accountability.** It is designed to improve your leadership skills when faced with crucial conversations that call for coaching, accountability, and corrective action. Practice, practice, practice the steps first with an associate and then keep refining your technique. With experience, your actual one-on-one sessions with team members will prove to be critically important in reinforcing your leadership standing and building more significant relationships with colleagues, in addition to increasing your organization's success.

CASA II Technique—Connecting as a Leader for Coaching and Accountability

This four-step process is a valuable tool that can result in leading more effective meetings that then translate into actions that achieve stronger relationships and greater results. **Improving levels of self-awareness, empathy, and listening skills are integrated in different phases of the process.**

A. Before the Meeting, Connect with Yourself.

Ask yourself:

1. How am I thinking and feeling about this meeting? Positive or negative? Why? Is it real or self-created bias, ego, etc.? See

it, feel it. Say, "I feel positive about my ability to help change people and situations based on my successful experiences and self- confidence.

2. What negative thoughts and emotions do I have about this colleague?

    a. Are they basically a good person?
    b. Are they trying to do the right thing?
    c. Are they doing things in a different way than I am?
    d. How can I be nonjudgmental? Stay nonjudgmental?

What do I think is their attitude about this meeting?

Am I being empathetic to their situation? Do they have personal issues they're dealing with that I need to take into account?

    a. What are the specific goals or results I want to achieve from this meeting?
    b. Are there barriers and challenges I need to overcome for a satisfying resolution?
    c. Are there areas we can compromise on? If so, which ones?

Am I going into this meeting with a "Growth Mindset," believing that setbacks and challenges are temporary, and there are learning experiences that lead to positive outcomes?

Next, before the actual meeting, put yourself in a Mindset for Success to connect with your colleague.

1. Be centered, present, relaxed, and optimistic about the conversation.
2. Be aware of your breathing patterns.
3. **Affirm** your commitment to remain open, flexible, nonjudgmental, respectful, and empathetic.

4. Remind yourself to keep eye contact and complete focus on your colleague's state of mind and react accordingly.

B. Start the Meeting

1. Say something positive related to their work: "Great job last week with that tough sales call."
2. Ask, "What's your thinking about the goal (issue or situation) that we need to address today?"
3. Ask, "How do you feel about this? Why do you feel this is happening?"
4. Ask, "What actions or changes do you think need to be made?"
5. Remind yourself to remain open, flexible, and collaborative. Ask, "Do we have any other options?"
6. Ask, "Do you have any more suggestions on ways we can make things even better?"
7. Ask, "How can I be of help to you? What other support would you like?"

C. Gain Agreement

Review and reaffirm the direction forward:

1. "Okay, so this is the action/change we both mutually agreed to do going forward. Right?"
2. "Again, why do you feel this will work? Do you really believe it's the right way to go?"
3. "I agree with you! So together let's make this action/change a success!"

CASA III TECHNIQUE—Building Stronger Relationships Through Self-Awareness, Trust, and Listening Skills

The third and final leg of the CASA Model focuses on three particular relationship-building qualities:

1. **Self-awareness.** Be present and aware of your thoughts, emotions, and actions.
2. **Trust.** Lead with honesty, empathy, and support.
3. **Listen. Be genuine, attentive, and inquisitive.**

   a. **Be genuine in wanting to connect and hear what the other person is saying.** Most important, remove ego-based issues from your thoughts. Be aware of your thoughts and feelings that might inhibit listening exactly to what the other person is saying.
   b. **Be attentive to what the other person is saying and do not offer a planned response.** Focus on what they are saying nonverbally to add more meaning to their spoken words.
   c. **Be inquisitive: question, question, question in short 30-second segments.** "Is this the point you're making?" Pause and rephrase their responses to clarify and truly understand their message. "How did you come to this conclusion? How do you feel about things? How can I help you?"
   d. **Use eye contact and body language to show your feelings**. Empathize and strive for the same genuine state (Neural Resonance) as the other person.
   e. **Additional listening techniques:**

      1. Don't interrupt.
      2. If at all possible, don't argue, criticize, or patronize.
      3. Regulate your emotional response.
      4. Observe your own and their body language.
      5. Listen with intuitiveness.

ACCOUNTABILITY

After the direction forward has been clarified and affirmed, set benchmarks for measuring progress on the agreement with your colleague.

1. Say, "This is what we agree to do then; you'll be taking these actions over the next (30, 60, 90 days). Right?" Pause for their confirmation.
2. Say, "Here's what I have agreed to do to support and help you. Okay?" Pause for their confirmation.
3. Say, "We'll meet again in two weeks to see if any progress has been made and to make sure you're moving in the right direction. Or if you need additional support. Do you agree?" Pause for their confirmation.
4. Say, "I feel very good about the actions you'll be taking. I am confident in your ability to make this all happen and to increase your success. Based on your skills and abilities and past performance, I feel the outcome will be even better than we planned."

POST MEETING REVIEW

After you have met with your colleague, make an assessment. Ask yourself:

1. "What happened positively or negatively at this meeting?"
2. "How did I handle the situation?"
3. "Did I empathize and really try to help the person?"
4. "Was I self-aware and listening effectively?"
5. "Did I grow from this experience? What did I learn?"
6. "What would I do differently next time?"

There is another leadership characteristic that is ever present and stands alone in the Mindset for Success Model and among the supporting techniques in the CASA Model: integrity.

This is true for several reasons. To start with, your credibility is central to how effectively you move in the world because your words and actions carry weight. With a reputation as a person who keeps his or her promises in good stead, it is easier to build relationships and thus gain more opportunity. People will respect you. They will listen to you. They will follow you.

Your integrity also serves in ways you might not readily think of. For example, think of yourself as a visionary leader. Integrity nurtures your clear mind, which is a necessary mindset for insightfulness. It frees your thinking to go beyond the confines of known variables and invites you to capitalize on as many unknowns as you can. And it can give you the vocabulary to effectively communicate your vision and enlist others to buy in.

Jim Collins, author of the international bestseller *Good to Great*, has a lot to say about this process of buying in. For starters, he recognizes that coming up with a vision is much easier than making it into a reality. Achieving that reality requires getting the right people on the bus, getting them sitting in the right seats, and then getting them to drive together to a specific destination.

So what is the process to get the right people in the right seats on the same bus? Or phrased differently, how do you refine your vision so that others take ownership of it too? One approach is to include them in the developmental stages. By allowing others to contribute and, in fact, help shape the vision, they inherently take on a sense of ownership precisely because they are personally invested—it is their baby too. With that commitment, success is much more likely.

This approach is a partnership, much like the leader/sales professional partnership I wrote about earlier. It leads the team to refer to it as "our vision." It's important then for a leader to create an environment where everybody's input is taken into account. And it's important for a leader to engage in a discussion about the why behind "our vision."

Getting to the why, especially when it concerns being visionaries, can be hard to nail down. Sometimes people say they have vision and that they know where they're going, but it's not clear to anybody else other than themselves. It is not enough to say, for example, "We want to increase our branch's sales to be the best in the region." Instead, a vision statement lays out, "We can increase our branch's sales to be the best in the region by establishing our-selves in the new business park a few exits past Chelsea, upgrading our sales software to HubSpot so we can automate follow-up emails and reminders, contacting new leads within twenty-four hours after receiving the referrals, giving comp time for a study hour each workday during April and May for anyone taking the licensing exam in June, and expanding incentive programs that will benefit the team's immediate family, and twice a year for one week open the incentive program to extended "Family and Friends."

Sales manager Tom Blake sees it this way: "I think a key is defi-nitely making sure that from day one you're communicating your vision for your organization and your core values and just con-stantly talking to people about where the organization is going. And I believe people want to be a part of something. If you're com-municating that message enough, you'll find the people who want to be a part of the growth of the organization. You've just got to be passionate about it from day one."

Richard Sear has a similar take with an emphasis on communi-cating a clear vision to his team while also trying to understand what it is the team wants to achieve. He talks about it in terms of aligning the two. He points out that this alignment process means people have to know what they want. Where do they want to go? What will make them happy? What is it they want to achieve? Reaching this clarity is often challenging and can take a lot of soul-searching and a collective melding of the minds. This give and take for mutual understanding helps build that sense of buying in, which in turn generates more success. Actually, Richard takes it a step further: "I want to give them complete ownership and help challenge them around their personal growth and around their ability to drive and impact results for what they are responsible."

This brings to view an important point about reaching your highest potential and pushing yourself beyond what you thought was possible. A good leader raises the bar continually through communicating with positive reinforcement and being open to the partnership concept.

Embracing a dynamic environment, helping others cope with change, and adapting and being flexible along with some consideration for a certain amount of standing still until the dust settles are hallmarks of good leadership. In fact, a person in charge who is waiting for change to happen instead of being a catalyst for change, particularly in the marketplace, sets themselves up to be on the defensive, especially with the rate of change accelerating so fast through more technology. They'll likely find themselves out of step, tied up in knots, and at best treading water. And unfortunately, their unpreparedness will hurt their team.

Adapting to change applies as well to self-leadership. For example, are you successfully prioritizing and then integrating the daily flood of information affecting your life and that of your loved ones? Are you taking the next much more difficult step of successfully updating your core values to remain true to yourself while also taking into account global changes toward women's rights, racial equality, economic justice, environmental protection, and so much more?

I hope your answer is yes. Because over the long haul, leadership of any kind requires constant learning and adapting to responsibilities with the resources you have, and a constant upholding of your core values.

In fact, we are in the midst of a worldwide shift toward the democratization of leadership. No longer is the power concentrated with just a few because entrepreneurs, consumer activists, social activists, and millions more at the grassroots level have gained, and continue to gain, more leverage over power. For example, a boycott started by one and multiplied by tens of thousands supporters can create a movement that is a force to be reckoned with. Case in point: the #DeleteUber campaign waged through Twitter and Facebook resulted in the ridesharing service losing a reported 200,000 customers and opening the way for competitor Lyft.

The best leaders recognize that centralized power around themselves is yesterday's news; we are in an age of the humble leader embracing the empowerment of others. The best leaders also understand that giving up more control and committing to empowering the rank and file serves the organization's mission. A direction needs to be communicated and reinforced by many voices—not just by the person with the big office. Everyone is equal in a humanistic way, and roles need to be carried out at different levels. They understand that climbing the ladder as best as they can is only part of their success and another part is taking other people with them.

John Maxwell is indeed a treasure trove of wisdom on leadership, and quite a prolific writer. In his book, *Everyone Communicates, Few Connect: What the Most Effective People Do Differently*, he discusses the concept of "spreading the wealth" to be more inclusive and how this action redefines what effective leadership is. He writes, "Poet, journalist, and editor Alan Ross asserted, 'Humility means knowing and using your strengths for the benefit of others, on behalf of a higher purpose. The humble leader is not weak . . . is not preoccupied with self, but with how best to use his or her strengths for the good of others. A humble leader does not think less of himself, but chooses to consider the needs of others in fulfilling a worthy cause. I love to be in the presence of a humble leader because they bring out the very best in me . . .' What a great perspective. False humility downplays one's genuine strengths to receive praise. Arrogance plays up one's strength to receive praise. Humility raises up others so they can be praised."

Part of this servant leader approach is leading by example. Joe Veilleux is one who recognizes this. He sees himself as a player coach, believes in his team, and works hard right beside them, helping them to be the best they can be. His team not only knows this about him, but they depend on his partnership. "I think you have to be inspiring because people want to be part of something that's great and sometimes they forget about that. So you've got to remind them, 'Remember the time when you did something where you were number one and you were the best at whatever that was—how did that make you feel?' My job is to get you to have that feeling every day and every year, because that's when you're happy."

Joe's commitment extends to emphasizing the importance of upholding personal values. "I want people to succeed, I want people to win. But you need to do it the right way. We are not going to sell someone something if they can't afford it and if they don't need it. I talk about that every time I do a new training class so they know this is an organization that doesn't jam sales down people's throats. They need to understand why they're buying it, they need to be able to afford it."

He adds, "I review sales upon submission. I'm going to make sure those sales make sense. Our team understands that and a lot of times they're not going to bring me cases they know I wouldn't approve—so they make that determination while still with the client. They'll say, 'Well ma'am, I don't see how you can afford this.' They'll tell people that."

In addition to integrity, there's another standard Joe always emphasizes: "When you have success, make a point to celebrate it. Even for a small success. Little victories can build one on top of the other until you have a larger accomplishment."

This esprit de corps is often contagious and then everybody can join in on the celebration and have some fun. They can feel good about helping one another get ahead. This moves the attitude in the office from a zero-sum game where there is only one winner and the rest lose out to having plenty of opportunities for everybody to be winners.

Take recruiting for example. It is a vital responsibility of an insurance sales manager to bring in new agents. Keith Lozowski believes recruiting is one of the most important things he does. So much so that he makes recruiting a consistently occurring part of the culture. That means all of the time, not just when there's pressure to meet recruitment goals. "It's not like if early on I recruited heavily and then I had a good class so maybe I can take my foot off the pedal."

No, because it doesn't matter if he had ten people just start or two people, he's recruiting with the same excitement and the same intensity fifty-two weeks a year. "We really don't take off a week, typically. We're just on every week. I look at it from an agent's perspective because agents need to be prospecting all the time. That's how they grow their business. The way we grow our business as managers is by recruiting."

You might be wondering if the new people being brought in ever upset the balance of relationships in Keith's office. Sure, at times. But that's why the way people are recruited and why having a broader culture where fresh faces are welcomed in and can find a place with new opportunities to provide for their families are so important.

For his agents already settled in place, these new recruits can be inspiring too. Keith knows that underneath those faces of determination and resilience, over the years, even veterans might find themselves struggling to keep their fire lit. They might even be questioning if they want to do this anymore. "I think they oftentimes get re-invigorated by the attitude and the excitement of a new agent. I just believe that by going out and meeting people and identifying personalities and strengths, you can find what peg to put where. I've always said that our job isn't to take square pegs and jam them in round holes; our job is to find a square peg and then put it in a square hole so that we have the right fit for the right person, and that's how our team succeeds."

So when he sits in front of a group of prospective new agents he tells them, "We are going to do everything we can to train you and teach you how to be successful in this business. I mean our whole team is going to do everything in our power. We're not going to fail you, if anything you're going to fail us. We talk about it all the time. We don't quit you, you quit us. As long as you've got the right attitude and the right effort, we're going to keep trying."

Getting started can be overwhelming for any new sales professional. Especially if it's your first year and you're on straight commission or even draw against commission, then you're most likely just trying to survive. Everyone goes through this process of being tested, so you can find some camaraderie with others who have been there for a while. I encourage you to ask them for advice. They'll probably tell you of their own struggles starting out—maybe how even today they can't stand the sight of macaroni and cheese because it reminds them of how they lived off that stuff back then. But they'll also likely tell you to keep trying and how your second year will be way better. And that by the third year, you'll be the one giving advice to some new guy just starting out. No matter how much seniority you have, your empathy helps you and everyone you touch to grow.

From your generosity of spirit to help comes greater opportunities in ways you might not even realize. For example, diving in and helping colleagues sends a message to the higher-ups at your company that you have potential to move up.

Here's how they think. First, they are going to look to make sure you have the passion to take on new responsibilities. Second and third, that you can sell and can train and inspire others to sell. In short, the leadership traits you demonstrate in managing your own client base need to be transferrable to a larger scale.

Another important factor is characterized by caring. I discussed earlier that your success in sales is dependent on genuinely caring about your clients—this also increasingly applies to your advancement as a leader. In the simplest language, true leaders care. They care about their work, their clients, and especially their team members.

They also recognize that their own pride can hinder the advancement of the team and its optimal performance. So they understand the value of giving up control and being more focused on empowering and developing team leaders to ultimately transform those relationships into partnerships.

Gary Downing adds a refreshing view of how he sees growing in leadership. "I believe that when you get an opportunity to lead people to go maybe one step past wherever they thought it was possible for them to go, that's an honor." Furthermore, he sees leadership not necessarily as a natural skill, but one that can be learned through making a commitment to excel, no matter what level you start at. "You have to want to keep growing in order to be an effective leader. And if you don't have the passion to grow, then others will see that and your influence will fall off."

He also has an interesting view of what leadership is at its heart. "It's about inspiring and not necessarily motivating." He believes if you can inspire, then the motivation will be a natural outcome. "Our job as leaders is to create an environment that people are attracted to, that they want to be a part of and that inspires them every day to be the very best that they can be. People will gravitate toward that type of leadership."

This approach of bringing out the best in others carries with it a lot of responsibility, particularly in keeping the team moving forward together. When times are good, enjoy and celebrate the victories and build on the successes. Push for more, compete harder, and raise your expectations. When times are tough, communicate what the situation is, then let them know the plan to navigate through the rough waters and that you've got their backs.

In Gary's words, "We're there with them. If an agent has a bad day or had a bad month or they're in a bad way of whatever nature, I get in the trenches with them and let them know that I care. I don't stand from afar and let them know how disappointing they are."

He is keenly aware that in his business "the only working asset that you have are your agents. ... As a leader of a branch, if you don't have any managers and you don't have any agents, you're not leading—you're just going for a walk" with nobody following you. So it is vital to stay connected with them, like a family.

Gary also is a believer in the "Strengthsfinder" philosophy developed by Tom Rath that I alluded to earlier. This approach emphasizes a person's strengths by putting them in situations where they can win. And to do that means a leader has to know not only his own strengths but the strengths of the team.

There was a time not that long ago when leadership models centered around identifying people's weaknesses and working to improve them. Certainly, it is still valuable to be well-rounded and to do what you can to achieve that. But honestly, everybody has shortcomings that can be improved, though it is also likely it will take a great amount of energy and resources to do so.

What the "Strengthsfinder" approach does is turn traditional thinking on its head. Gary identifies a person's strengths and puts them in positions where they can shine. "I think it's important to know each team member's strengths and weaknesses so that you can grow them in the area that they're strong and really prevent them from continually getting tripped up in the areas where they're weak."

Gary's other thoughts on leadership deal with the fundamentals and are relevant in any organization. They begin with his expectations of the people he works with. First, he wants them to care. Second, he wants them to be driven. Third, he wants them to be challenged. Fourth, he wants them to do their best. And fifth, he wants them to think about their legacy—how far they will advance until they eventually pass the baton on to those coming up.

For Gary, leadership is a privilege that is earned "by doing things right and by doing things well. And don't take for granted the privilege that you've been given. Embrace it, grow with it, reach out, get help when you need it and aspire to do great things."

Neal Quimby likes to tell about the changes he has undergone with his leadership skills. It's not as if he learned one style and stuck with it forever. He has had to keep growing and adapting. "I can tell you that when I first moved into a leadership role, I was very directive. But over the years, I've developed into a better leader in the sense that I've looked at colleagues as partners, looked at empowering people, looked at relationships and I've also looked at accountability. So I do more pulling versus pushing."

Just as Neal, Gary, and other outstanding leaders I have had the pleasure of working with have done, you too can customize the Mindset for Success Model for the most genuine fit with your unique personality.

The most essential piece of advice I can give you about leadership is to be yourself. By being authentic, you will have a far greater impact on those relying on you for guidance. You'll become a greater inspiration to many, even to people you might consider to be outside your circle of influence, and you'll become more effective in reaching your goals. When you embrace a culture of genuineness, humbleness, and service, you will find yourself to be the leader you have strived to become.

Lesson Learned

Leadership is a "contact sport" in the sense that you are persuading, influencing others to change a point of view, reach mutual agreement, or take action. Though there is no set formula for leadership, there are a number of commonly held strengths that consistently show up among great leaders. Those qualities include adeptness at developing a positive environment, being genuinely caring, being a good listener, being a good example to follow, and being a person of integrity. These characteristics along with Neural Resonance have been incorporated into the **CASA III TECHNIQUE—Building Stronger Relationships Through Self-Awareness, Trust, and Listening Skills** for you to use and modify for your greater success.

There are many other traits that are unique to you, like having a good sense of humor or being consistently calm and focused, that can contribute to making you into a solid leader. Find your own path by accentuating your strengths. Discover what you're best at, then work to bring out the best in others. All the while, continue to improve yourself in areas that show promise.

Chapter 8
The Measure of Success

The Mindset for Success Model offers insight into measuring your success. For example, rather than seeing yourself as competing with others, the most gifted sales professionals and leaders focus more on competing with themselves. They know the best is within and so access their excellence by staying true to their core values.

Lori Moncada shares this same view about success as uniquely individual, personal, and defined by her own terms, not by anyone else's. "I love what I do, and I'm committed to it. I'm disciplined. It's a part of my life. It's not that I do this and then I go home. It's what I do and it's now who I am, and that's something that bolsters my success." For her, loving her work is a measure of success regardless of the outcome. "I think I describe success on any level as actually being happy and loving where I'm at. I don't really measure success monetarily. I reach goals. Though I don't always reach my goals. But I think the real questions for me are, 'Am I happy? Do I love where I'm at?' So, that's where success lies for me."

Making a difference in people's lives is another meaningful measure of success. How much grace you carry yourself with, how well you get along with others, and how composed you remain even under duress are other ones. It's important to add these "others" onto the scale to counterbalance the tendency to just look at money and power as the success-determining heavyweights. By framing your view of yourself in this more global perspective and by looking at yourself as a caring, hardworking, and conscientious person, you can enjoy new levels of a successful career.

Gary Downing thinks about success this way: "It is important on a regular basis that you take an inventory of your strengths and talents, but do not confuse them with the gifts that you have been given. See, strengths and talents are what you do on a regular basis to achieve certain tasks and goals and yes, they are crucial to develop for your continued success. But to me, understanding your gifts is what really impacts people and makes this a better world to live in.

"I believe that success is really about setting forth to do your absolute very best—being able to overcome the obstacles that are presented to you and never giving up. Whatever that looks like at the end, as long as you can look back and say, 'I have no regrets, I gave it my all and did the best that I could.' I believe that's success."

What's interesting about Gary's thinking is he has in fact been number one and remains consistently near the top. So it isn't that he traded in his edge to find some warm feelings. His approach actually has kept him clearheaded so he can continue to achieve. "Number one is awesome and winning does matter. And I think everybody should aspire to win. But again, winning's different for everybody and I would never say that someone who gave their absolute very best and fell short is a loser by any stretch."

Neal Quimby echoes a similar viewpoint. "I believe that success isn't determined by how many challenges you have. It's determined by how you overcome each and every one of them. Because the reality is, as you start down the road to success, there are going to be challenges. It doesn't matter what you're doing for a profession or what company you're working for, there are going to be challenges."

TJ Bean sees his success largely in terms of honoring a commitment to hold himself accountable for his professional and personal philosophy to serve. He insists on disciplined thinking to drive forward, to push through distractions and obstacles, and to achieve his goals with integrity. And he keeps raising the bar on himself. "Successful people do what people who are unsuccessful don't. Success is making hard choices to do the right thing for good people. If you're constantly doing that, and you're making it a priority in your business, you'll never go wrong."

There are many guidelines for success as described throughout this book that I encourage you to use as they are or to personalize as you wish. Stripped bare, there is no one-size-fits-all Holy Grail for success. You are unique and ultimately it is up to you to blaze your own trail.

In Their Own Words
Success Stories from Sales Professionals and Leaders

Denny Riley, Sales Leader
Cedar Falls, Iowa

I started with my company on February 15, 1985. I was twenty-nine, no college, no nothing, and failing miserably in the insurance business in a little town in northeast Iowa. About 1,200 people lived there at the time. My wife and I had a baby at eighteen. Then we had a set of twins at twenty-one. Before this, my first job was in a factory for a while. All my family worked in factories building tractors. I did it for about six months and couldn't take it. It was just killing me, so I actually left. I had a brand-new baby and I left. I went into selling vacuum cleaners, knocking door to door, on strict commission. Of course, my family thought I'd lost my mind and my father-in-law wanted to shoot me. I sold vacuums, sold cars, and then sold insurance. It's funny, even now to this day—my hometown's only an hour from here—my agents will go up to my hometown and work and they'll come back and they laugh. They'll say, "We just talked to somebody that bought a vacuum cleaner from you, bought a car from you and bought insurance from you." So I got into the insurance business and it was basically the normal insurance story. I had absolutely no training. I called on my friends and relatives. Basically, once I went through my friends and relatives, I really didn't know what else to do because I had no training.

Then one day, it was hotter than hell. It was like a hundred and some degrees outside. My wife worked part-time at a grocery store in this little town. There was no place to work, but this guy was nice enough to give her a part-time job. I'm home with the kids in the middle of the afternoon and there's a knock at my door. This guy knocks, I answer the door and the guy goes, "Mr. Prodee?"

I'm like, "No, Prodee lives across the street."

He goes, "My name's Vern Whitney and I work for—"

"I'm like, 'Oh yeah, I sell insurance too.'"

"Alright then I'll come back and talk to you."

It was hot. I had no place to go. I'm a loser, so I'm waiting at home babysitting my three kids. And he came back and talked to me, and that's how I found my way. A guy knocked on the wrong door. That's how I came to a sales career and great success.

I had no desire to stay in the insurance business. We were broke. My father-in-law had bought a little-bitty house and let us live there with no rent. We had a garden. That's where we got our food. My wife's dad farmed. He gave us meat. We had nothing. My family saved all their bottles and cans to give us so we could get back the deposit money, so we could take the kids to get a treat. The whole nine yards.

So I had three kids already when I started. The guy that hired me was Bob Ward. He just passed away about a year ago. He was my all-time favorite person in the entire world. Bob would drive an hour every day to pick me up and take me to work because he knew I didn't have the money for gas. He and his wife would grab steaks and lobsters and come to our house and grill them out because we had never had lobster before. The whole nine yards.

My branch was in Cedar Falls. But they had a big regional thing in Des Moines. Anyway, we had to go down to a meeting in Des Moines. My wife was going down with me and she said, "Do they pay for a hotel room?"

"God, I hope so."

She goes, "What happens if they don't?"

"I guess we sleep in the car." Then we get down there and they say, "Of course we pay your hotel room. A room's been reserved for you."

Anyway, we had three little girls, and that's when Cabbage Patch dolls were really popular. My little girls would always be dreaming about having Cabbage Patch dolls. They had cutouts from magazines of Cabbage Patch dolls. There was just no way we could afford the cost—they were 35 bucks apiece. There was no way. We couldn't spend $35 a week for groceries, let alone for a doll.

About six months later we had to go back down to Des Moines again, and things were way different by then. Things were rolling. We were making some money. It was back in early '86. On the way back, we drove through this town and there was a Target store. We stopped there to get some stuff and just as we stopped, they were unloading a shipment of Cabbage Patch dolls. I walked past these Cabbage Patch dolls and I stopped and I grabbed three of them. My wife was like, "Are you kidding me?" I'm like, "Nope." I go up to the counter and the gal says, "That'll be $105." She looks at me and I'm crying like a baby. I look over and my wife's crying. Of course, the gal behind the counter's like, "What the hell?" I spent $105 for Cabbage Patch dolls. All the way home we were crying. We were just like, "Oh my God, this is the greatest company in the world." Something dumb like that. Just things like that are what's kept me through—those are the stories you remember when times get rough.

Just a few months after that, I took my first branch and we moved to Omaha, Nebraska. My first branch was in Omaha. Now I'm a branch manager in Cedar Falls and we're booming. I feel like I've been really blessed with the successful career I've had and I just want to make everyone around me successful too.

I just had a conversation about this all with my agents the other day. It takes a lot of effort to be successful. It's way easier to be a loser than it is to be a winner. Anybody can be a loser, right? It's a piece of cake. But **changing the mindset** I had, accepting being a piece of crap, basically, and not making any money and living off my father-in-law. We even had food stamps once and my wife was so embarrassed in the grocery store. She came home and she goes, "I don't care if we starve to death. I'm never doing this again."

Then I finally got to the point where I'm saying to myself, "It is embarrassing. I'm embarrassed by the car I drive. I'm embarrassed by the house I live in. I'm embarrassed that I can't take my family to McDonald's, for Christ's sake." But I just never thought there was ever going to be an opportunity. Then I found my way in sales and all of a sudden, I'm telling myself, "Hell, you can do whatever you want. You can accomplish whatever you want."

Lesson Learned

Denny's story reminds each of us that you have a choice in how you want your life to be. By guiding your thoughts, staying true to your beliefs, and creating your Mindset for Success, you can determine your level of success and fulfillment in life. Your healthy "Beliefs" will impact your "Emotions," which will then lead you to taking the needed "Actions" to make a difference.

Trisa Jackson, Sales Professional
Tacoma, Washington

I don't have a strong academic background. I didn't graduate from college. My background is in singing, theater, and entertainment. I married my high school sweetheart and we both had musical talents so we set out to light the world on fire. We traveled to New York City and were entertainers in several Broadway musicals. From there we were successful singers and entertainers on cruise ships for many years. Eventually, though, we listened to the call to return home to Tacoma and settle down.

My first job back was as a waitress at a bar. Then, as fate would have it, I met someone in outside sales named Sally Colley Allen. Sally both encouraged me and had frank conversations with me about my future. She said, "What are you doing here? You can make over $100,000 a year doing what I do." So, at age thirty-two, with Sandy mentoring me, I took the plunge and joined Gary Downing's branch office. Gary had a huge influence on me. He taught me about team selling and individual accountability. He taught me that failure is not an option.

All the while, I kept saying to myself, *how funny is it for me to be here. I never thought I'd be doing this. Sales? I'm not even good at math.* I worked hard. Results were slow in coming, but I enjoyed helping people. I really wanted to help my customers. It was a real calling for me. A mission.

When I started, I was also amazed and surprised that there were colleagues with all sorts of backgrounds that came from all walks of life, had little or no more education than myself, and were what I considered extremely successful in capturing the American Dream. I indeed am living that life today because of my success in sales.

So whereas I didn't have a lot of confidence or faith in my abilities at first, there was always that nagging question in the back of my head, "Why not me?" The more I learned, the more confidence I gained. I used my background and life experiences to teach others, including my clients.

At first, I was embarrassed when a client would ask, "What is your background?" and I would say, "cruise ship singer." But soon, the thing that I heard from my clients repeatedly over the years is that I am different from most financial advisors. I don't make things complicated. I don't talk over their heads. For the first time they had someone sit down with them and it actually made sense what I was explaining.

I believe this is due to the fact that I struggled to learn the information myself. It didn't come easily or naturally. Like Sir Richard Branson and many other successful entrepreneurs, I too had personal challenges. To overcome this, I would overprepare. I would take things slower or break them down to the basics. I am very visual so I will write things out, draw pictures, and tell stories that explain the situation in a different light. From my years singing on cruise ships, I learned that when making a mistake in front of hundreds of people, it's only a big deal if you make it a big deal. If you forget the words in the middle of a song, just be quiet and start mouthing the word "watermelon." The audience will think that there is something wrong with your mic and that the sound guy messed up! You just have to learn to go with the flow. You end up being all things to the people you help. You are their guide, their advisor, their daughter, their mother, sometimes their shrink, and hopefully always their friend.

I do enjoy the stories and the wisdom that my clients share with me. Everyone has a story to tell and sometimes it's just about being there to listen. It is not always easy and is often frustrating, but it is an honor and blessing to do what I do.

Lesson Learned

Trisa's story highlights that people from all walks of life can be successful at selling. That with time and practice, you can build the confidence needed to take charge of your sales career. And that it's okay to make mistakes. In fact, stepping into the unknown and learning from setbacks, then applying that new knowledge is a natural part of the process for greater success. Her story also reinforces the pivotal importance of being self-aware and nonjudgmental, as well as the importance of building strong relationships, and, finally, feeling that your work has meaning.

Penny Jones, Sales Professional
Philadelphia, Pennsylvania

I've had my share of hurdles in life. My husband was a carpenter and fell off a roof and got seriously injured. He went into intensive care and never really recovered from the fall, then passed away not long after from complications. That was when I was thirty-six and was left to raise our two young boys on my own. We hadn't done a lot of our own financial planning, so I didn't have much to lean back on. My parents helped a lot, thank God. So I decided I better go back to school and get some kind of training to take care of my family. I became a teacher, but it didn't turn out that well for me. Besides the work itself, financially it wasn't enough and my parents couldn't keep helping. After that I struggled to find my place until finally at age fifty-five, I was introduced to my company. The managers in the Philadelphia office really supported my development. Fortunately, I've become a top producer and it's changed my life and that of my kids. My kids are in their twenties now and both are in college.

After you've had as many hard knocks in life like I've had, you learn to trim the fat and get down to what's really important. So I'd say I'm all about living my values. I really want to help my clients. I believe in having meaningful conversations with them, not some kind of pushy sales approach. I believe in listening to them and showing empathy. Maybe for me it's a little different because I'm in the same age group as many of the other boomers I call on. Basically, they're my peers, so I can relate to them. The same is true for single mothers raising families and being the sole providers. I relate to them well too.

I see my role as being that of an educator. I go into a sales call and I educate the client. But I want to emphasize it's really a back and forth conversation. I don't pressure. This has worked out well for me in my seven years with my company and these days most of my business comes from referrals. And I take the day off on Fridays a lot.

There are things that I think about to help me with driving forward. Like I believe in Bill Lombardo's Mindset for Success Model. It helps me process my thoughts and feelings and channel them into being more productive. It has also helped me find deeper meaning in my work through staying true to my values. And through appreciating the grit it takes to survive and flourish in this world. I look at a lot of women who are single mothers, and other women too, and really am a cheerleader for them. They're like quiet heroes raising families and looking out for others.

The heart of my business is customer service. The way I define customer service is reaching out on a consistent basis to my customer base and helping them with non-sales issues for the most part. Some of it is informational and some of it is service-related. Either way, I constantly emphasize the importance of customer service.

Lesson Learned

Penny's story reinforces that a flow of inspiration can come just from seeing your work as a mission to help your clients, largely through empathizing with them. It also emphasizes the role that having grit plays in your success so that you can take the challenges life gives you, get up, and keep moving forward. Like so many others who have had to handle it all, you too can persevere while staying true to your values.

Farshad Asl, Sales Leader
Los Angeles, California

I arrived in America, October 1998, with $400.00 in my pocket and a deep desire to transform my life. Even though I was in a foreign land, lacking connections and prospects, I knew I was going to make my "American Dream" a reality. I paid no attention to obstacles. I did not allow them to become an excuse against my success. I kept my dream alive.

If anyone had excuses for not succeeding in America, it would certainly be me. I didn't know the language, I wasn't familiar with the culture, I didn't have the possessions to create the "American lifestyle," and the list of possible excuses went on and on. But, I knew I had to move forward, I knew I needed to find a job and make a life for myself.

I knew that my biggest obstacle was going to be learning better English. I barely spoke it, but I refused to let that stop me. I was fully aware that I could easily fall prey to the plentitude of excuses for not making it in America. So I needed to be even more aware and intentional about making my success a reality. I simply did what needed to be done. At the time, the only English books I had with me were the Bible, a dictionary, and John C. Maxwell's *21 Laws of Leadership*. So, with those, I began to study the language and look for a job.

One morning I was sitting at the kitchen table with my wife, Mina, flipping through the help wanted section of the newspaper. The majority of the openings required experience and language skills that I didn't have. I was an independent businessman and mushroom farmer in Iran. I didn't know how that would translate into measurable success here.

After a long and tedious search, I came across an advertisement for a sales position. I discussed the potential and possibility of the position with Mina and received wonderful encouragement from her. She reminded me of my purpose and passion in life: that is to add value to the lives of others. As a salesman, I knew I would be able to work closely with people.

I still had the obstacle of not speaking English well, but paid no mind to it. The job was appealing to me, even though the details were a bit unclear. Nevertheless, I signed up for an interview and calmed my nerves about my thick accent.

After the briefing and interview, I learned the job was fundamentally about prospecting and marketing one's self. All the odds seemed to be against me, but I took the job anyway. I promised myself I was going to succeed no matter what. No excuses! Since I didn't have any connections or prospects to help me kick-start my business, my only resort was direct phone call sales. Cold calls!

"Hello, my name is Farshad, and—"

Click.

With each *click*, discouragement loomed over me like a dark cloud. But no matter how many times I was hung up on, I kept going because the only way to get appointments was to make the calls. By the end of the third day of cold calling, I was nearing nine hundred calls without as much as a full conversation. Something was definitely wrong, except I wasn't quite sure what.

Witnessing my troubles, Mina offered to help. We began rehearsing the phone script together. Perhaps the secret to all my troubles laid within it.

"Hello, my name is Farshad, and—"

Mina interrupted me at the same moment I would usually be hung up on. What were the chances of such a coincidence? She had realized something I couldn't ever have realized on my own. She suggested that perhaps the foreign nature of my name was a deterrent. Mina suggested that I take on an American version of my name, to help familiarize myself with my prospects. I could become Fred Asl. Maybe this change would bring success.

"Fred" is of course a far more acceptable and approachable name. I'm sure Mina was onto something, but my intentions were to build a successful brand with my name as Farshad Asl, not Fred Asl. In that moment, I realized my true intentions. I was going to keep making calls until I got appointments. I didn't directly know HOW all this would happen but I knew WHY it needed to happen.

The very next day as I began to make the calls, I concentrated on the purpose of my calling versus the words of the phone script. I worked on my diction so my name would be easier to understand. I summoned every ounce of my courage and confidence and said: "Hello, I'm FARSHAD ASL. I would like to talk to you about . . ."

After making more than nine hundred consecutive calls without even getting past the first part of my presentation, finally this time around I was able to successfully get through the whole introductory script. There was silence on the other end of the line. I feared I might have just missed the *click*! Did they already hang up on me? Then to my wonderful surprise the woman whom I called spoke up.

"Young man, I have absolutely no idea what you are talking about; I couldn't understand what you were saying. But if you want, I suppose we can set a time for you to come see me, so you can explain yourself face-to-face."

Now that I had successfully made my first appointment with such a gracious woman, it was time to move on to my next challenge, giving a full in-person presentation. Would my accent hinder the woman's comprehension? As I drove out to the appointment, I was shaking with both nerves and excitement.

The woman was in her early seventies, extremely pleasant, and delightfully warm. She was very welcoming and was actually pleased that I had come to meet with her. Driven by excitement, I gave her a hello hug. When we got past the small talk, I explained my challenge with English, and asked her, "Can we read the brochure together?" With a warm smile, she said, "Okay, let's go for it."

While reading the brochure together we discussed its contents. We marked on the brochure the parts that struck her personally as the most important information. That day, I gained as much as she did out of the presentation. My experience with this kind woman erased any excuse I could ever use against myself. She gave me a reason to believe in myself. She gave me confidence. I knew what I was capable of achieving. She gave me the hope that I needed.

What I gained from that first encounter set my feet upon the path that I follow to this day. She has positively impacted my life and career. With her influence, I was able to grow personally and professionally and went on to make many more appointments and sales.

Years later I transitioned to where I am now as a regional sales director where I oversee more than twenty different offices. All I needed was that defining moment to believe in myself and to realize there is no excuse ever worth giving.

Lesson Learned

Farshad's story is the American story. Barely able to speak English and facing all kinds of obstacles as an immigrant, he proves that through an unwavering belief in yourself and through helping others, you can have the life you aspire toward and at the same time make a difference in the lives of others. His story also raises the question, "What is really holding you back from the life you want?"

Tee Khan, Sales Professional
Wichita, Kansas

I attribute a lot of my success as a salesperson to modeling successful sales professionals—especially how they handle disappointments and setbacks. From them, I learned to grieve. Sometimes it takes a few hours. Sometimes shorter or longer. Through that process, I tell myself it's in the past, to put the setback behind me, and to get right back up. I find that how quickly I accept the reality of a negative situation the quicker I can move forward again. Through self-talk and self-questioning, I have been able to put this process into my everyday discipline. I realize this self-talk mindset is a major factor in my success and am grateful for those who have mentored me in this approach. Now, I mentor countless other colleagues in the same way. In fact, there is now a network, a support system, in my office. "Don't Panic, Don't Give Up" is our guiding principle.

My real success stories are not about making huge commissions but are more about helping clients and their families. Here is one story.

I had an evening appointment in the fall of 1988. I was a second-year financial planning agent, so relatively new, and when I saw that beautiful house I got discouraged. I even thought about not going in for the meeting—then I reminded myself, "This lady is waiting for me and I told her I would be there on time." So I wanted to be honorable and say hello to her, give her my business card, and let her know that if she wanted to talk about any concerns to call me.

When she opened the door, she was very courteous and hospitable and invited me in. I gave my "call me when you need me speech" and she asked whether I could compare all of her Medicare supplements (back then one could buy several of them). After I recommended keeping only one and canceling the others, she was comforted. She was delighted to know that she could save money. I asked a lot of questions during my stay and left two hours later with a check for $150,000 to be put in an annuity. In the next six years, I collected over $500,000 for annuities and helped her with life insurance too. I became her sister and son's agent as well. She was a retired schoolteacher. Teachers in general save more than other professionals.

There's also another story. I was meeting with existing clients to review their financial planning. As I was updating their files, they told me of their concern about their only daughter's upcoming divorce. After asking several questions, together we identified their biggest fear was if they died tomorrow, would their soon-to-be ex-son-in-law take half of their assets that they were leaving for their daughter? I knew that this was an estate-planning issue and that it would really make them relieved if they could sit down with a specialist.

Since they did not know any estate attorneys, I suggested they call one I'd worked with and arrange a meeting at no cost. The end result was after about three weeks, they had a trust set up so that their daughter would receive an inheritance protected from any creditors, including the divorcing spouse. They also applied for a large life insurance policy to enhance funding that trust on a tax-free basis. I realized afterward that once we found out what was on their minds, then the solution was easy.

Lesson Learned

Tee's story validates the approach that continually developing personally and professionally holds the key to your best possible quality of life. Though clearly this does not come easily for most, with persistent adherence to values that emphasize being honorable, being of service, and being resilient, you too can achieve success, both in terms of meaningfulness and financial reward.

Kareem Aboul-hosn, Sales Leader
Clearwater, Florida

I was born in Louisville, Kentucky, and moved to Lebanon when I was two. It's a war-torn country and I have memories of both its beauty and of its devastation. My parents emigrated back to the United States when I was a teenager. They were very hardworking people and I think that I learned from them how important it is to stay focused, keep driving forward, and never give up. They wanted me to go into the family business of running franchise restaurants throughout the state of Florida, but I felt drawn toward outside sales.

So after college, I signed on. It was very difficult for me at first. And to be honest it had something to do with the political environment. This was right after 9/11 and with a name like Kareem, you can imagine I got a frosty response from a lot of people. In many ways I can't blame them. It was a time with a lot of fear and uncertainty.

I kept at it, though, and eventually became very successful. I had a lot of motivation. Mostly I wanted to prove to myself and to my parents that I could be a role model and do things to help people. Even though I was having success, my parents still questioned why I would work on straight commission. But their doubts only made me double my efforts to be more successful. I did this mostly through understanding that I needed to be there for my clients. I needed to listen to them and anticipate their needs.

A turning point for me came when I was promoted to being a field trainer. By taking on responsibility for helping others sell, that gave me more confidence to become a better leader. I worked hard at mentoring them and found this work very fulfilling. I made some mistakes along the way of course. But I used those as learning experiences and became a better person for having come through those setbacks. One thing I learned very clearly was to not take shortcuts. There were so many others dependent on me that I really made a deliberate choice to follow my company's system. On top of that, the culture in the company of being caring and supportive really helped me personally, and I saw it also helped so many more in their development too.

Then I moved to Charlotte, North Carolina, and worked with great people. I had excellent mentors who helped me focus even more on my personal and professional development. We had great success together and drove our team to new heights. That led to me being promoted to sales manager of the Clearwater, Florida, office.

It was a real challenge for me, I have to admit. But I was determined to honor my family's name. And I had a lot of support and encouragement from people who each in their own way reached out to me during those difficult periods to make me feel included.

They helped me feel like an equal, as well as believe that I would rise to a higher level of performance and success.

They challenged me on the quality of my leadership team. "Are these the players that can lead you to greater success?" As a result, one of the first things I did was recruit a higher quality of leader and reorganize the team to create more of a servant leadership culture. This really reflected what I was all about and created a stronger team commitment to a high level of integrity and accountability.

It continues to work well with my own vision to be a humble and supportive leader. Overall, I feel that I am living the American Dream.

Lesson Learned

Kareem's story reinforces that, through consistent self-awareness and core values, you can overcome almost any challenge. Even if you started shortly after 9/11 in sales and cold-calling with a name like Kareem Aboul-hosn. But Kareem made the decision to not change his name, knowing full well that his sales would be affected. Instead he placed his values first to be able to understand why others had fears, what their concerns were about doing business with him, and how they could come to see his individual character. This decision to pursue his career on his terms despite the challenges speaks volumes about how essential grit is to rise to high levels of success.

SUGGESTED FURTHER READING

The following are books that help provide more in-depth knowledge and science to support a multiyear study in which I profiled, interviewed, and assessed the very best sales professionals and leaders. I encourage you to read these for developing your own professional sales and leadership skills.

Achor, Shawn. *The Happiness Advantage.* Crown 2010.

Andrews, Vidi, Jacobs, Randi, and Peterson, Peter P. *Executive Functions and the Frontal Lobes.*

Psychology Press 2008.

Cathcart, Jim. *Relationship Selling.* Perigee 1990.

Chopra, Deepak. *Soul of the Leader.* Harmony 2010.

Chopra, Deepak, and Tanzi, Rudy. *Super Brain.* Harmony 2012.

Chopra, Deepak, and Tanzi, Rudy. *Super Genes.* Harmony 2015.

Cohen, William A. *Drucker on Leadership.* Wiley 2009.

Collins, Jim. *Good to Great.* HarperBusiness 2001.

Colvin, Geoff. *Talent Is Overrated.* Portfolio 2008.

Duckworth, Angela. *Grit.* Scribner 2016.

Dweck, Carol. *Mindset.* Random House 2006.

Goulston, Mark. *Just Listen.* AMACOM 2009.

Greenberg, Cathy, and North, TC. *Fearless Leaders.* Waterfront 2014.

Hanke, Stacey, and Steinberg, Mary. *Yes You Can!* AuthorHouse 2008.

Helmstetter, Shad. *The Power of Neuroplasticity.* CreateSpace 2014.

Lakhiani, Vishen. *The Code of the Extraordinary Mind.* Rodale 2016.

Maxwell, John. *Everyone Communicates, Few Connect.* Thomas Nelson 2010.

Newberg, Andrew, and Waldman, Robert. *Words Can Change Your Brain.* Avery 2012.

Pink, Daniel. *A Whole New Mind.* Riverhead 2005.

Pink, Daniel. *Drive.* Riverhead 2009.

Pink, Daniel. *To Sell Is Human.* Riverhead 2012.

Ryback, David, Cathcart, Jim, and Nour, David. *ConnectAbility.* McGraw-Hill 2009.

Scott, Susan. *Fierce Conversations.* Penguin 2002.

Sinek, Simon. *Start with WHY, How Great Leaders Inspire Everyone to to Take Action.* Portfolio/Penguin 2009.

Sinek, Simon. *Find Your WHY.* Portfolio/Penguin 2017.

Whitmore, John. *Coaching for Performance.* Nicholas Brealey 2009.

Let's Connect

If you have a story to tell, professional sales and leadership techniques to share, feedback on this book, or are interested in Mindset for Success consultations and speaking engagements, please connect with me at BLombardo.com. At this website you'll also be able to order and access no-cost additional resources including workbooks, podcasts, and updates.

Acknowledgments

I'd like to take this opportunity to thank the special people that helped and supported me and, most important, reinforced my passion to carry on through my journey of discovery in writing my first book. I'm eternally grateful to them.

First and most important, I deeply appreciate and am thankful for Dr. Cathy Greenberg. Cathy's encouragement and coaching were vital to me as we both studied, tested, profiled, and observed the WHYs of what makes sales professionals and leaders successful in their everyday work. Without Cathy, there simply would be no book.

My partnership with my cowriter Kenneth Kales was a perfect match for me. Kenneth was calm, reassuring, and understanding while helping me search for my own voice and, once found, to then express it truthfully.

Also, the guy that kept me going during the fourth quarter was Jon Tota, CEO of Edulence. He was there for me with so much creativity and marketing savvy. Thank you Jon!

Dr. Glenn Boseman was a special partner who opened my vision to a greater professional audience that could directly benefit in a major way from the Mindset for Success Model and its supporting tools and practices.

Other colleagues that provided direct or indirect support along the way were Neal Quimby, Farshad Asl, Scott Perry, Mike Vietri, John Schrieffer, Scott Goldberg, Mike Buckley, Ed Berube, and Athina Mercuriou.

The important things in life always start and stop with one's family and I am truly blessed! My partner Danielle is the perfect match for me: giving me critical support, stark feedback, and the freedom and space to pursue my passion. Danny is the heart of our family and especially so for our kids, Max and Gaby. They're simply the best! I have learned so much from them. Max and Gaby truly have given great meaning to our lives.

It's also important for me to honor my parents, Joe and Angie. They gave to my sisters and brothers—Marlene, Joyce, John, Nick, and Joe—and me a zest and passion for life. We came from humble beginnings on the east side of Cleveland. We kids didn't have much but didn't know it then since my Mom and Dad gave us everything we really needed.

It seems so amazing how certain people appear at critical moments and play transformative roles that help in determining the direction of our lives. The most important juncture for me occurred in my junior year at Eastlake North High School in Ohio where home economics teacher Mrs. Marylou Manning was in charge of our study hall. Mrs. Manning believed in me before I really believed in myself. She encouraged me to run for senior class president, sold my dad on me going to college (I wasn't a very good student), and wrote inspiring letters to me when I was a student at Ohio University and Syracuse University. I was fortunate indeed to have the kind of teacher that every student needs and hopes for. Thank you so, so very much, Mrs. Manning, for your belief in me!

Finally, I want to extend a special thank-you to all the successful sales professionals and leaders that I interviewed, studied, and profiled in this book. I really appreciate you sharing your stories. It was a humbling experience to hear what people have had to overcome in many cases, and how through hard work and GRIT they are now living the American Dream.

At times during the past five years while writing *The American Dream Is a Mindset*, I questioned myself: *Why exactly am I doing this?* And the answer that always surfaced was a relentless inner spirit to give back. To help others as so many have helped me in my career and personal development. In these uncertain times we're living in, the proven models and techniques in this book can be especially helpful for being more centered and effective in your work and for living a more fulfilling life.